Foul Deeds and Suspicious Deaths Around Bedford

TRUE CRIME FROM WHARNCLIFFE

Foul Deeds and Suspicious Deaths Series

Staffordshire and The Potteries
Colchester
Manchester
Guildford
Derby
Northampton
Pontefract and Castleford
Tees
Bedford
Bristol
Carlisle
Newcastle
Southend-on-Sea
Barnsley
Birmingham
Blackburn and Hyndburn
Chesterfield
Coventry
Ealing
Guernsey
Huddersfield
Leeds
Liverpool
Newport
Nottingham
Rotherham
London's East End
Wigan

More Foul Deeds Wakefield
Mansfield
Leicester
Stratford and South Warwickshire
Brighton
Folkestone and Dover
Oxfordshire
Black Country
Durham
Bradford
Cambridge
Halifax
Scunthorpe
Barking, Dagenham & Chadwell Heath
Bath
More Foul Deeds Birmingham
Bolton
More Foul Deeds Chesterfield
Croydon
Grimsby
Hampstead, Holborn and St Pancras
Hull
Lewisham and Deptford
London's West End
Norfolk
Portsmouth
Warwickshire
York

OTHER TRUE CRIME BOOKS FROM WHARNCLIFFE

Norfolk Mayhem and Murder
The A-Z of London Murders
Unsolved Murders in Victorian and
    Edwardian London
Unsolved Yorkshire Murders
A-Z Yorkshire Murder
Brighton Crime and Vice 1800-2000
Essex Murders

Executions & Hangings in Newcastle
    and Morpeth
Norwich Murders
Unsolved Norfolk Murders
Yorkshire's Murderous Women
Black Barnsley
Durham Executions
Strangeways Hanged

Please contact us via any of the methods below for more information
or a catalogue.

WHARNCLIFFE BOOKS

47 Church Street – Barnsley – South Yorkshire – S70 2AS
Tel: 01226 734555 – 734222 Fax: 01226 – 734438
E-mail: enquiries@pen-and-sword.co.uk
Website: www.wharncliffebooks.co.uk

Foul Deeds & Suspicious Deaths Around

BEDFORD

Kevin Turton

Series Editor
Brian Elliott

Wharncliffe Books

First published in Great Britain in 2007 by
Wharncliffe Local History
an imprint of
Pen & Sword Books Ltd
47 Church Street
Barnsley
South Yorkshire
S70 2AS

ISBN 978 1 84563 028 7

Typeset in Plantin and Benguiat by
Phoenix Typesetting, Auldgirth, Dumfriesshire

Printed and bound in England by
Biddles Ltd, King's Lynn

Pen & Sword Books Ltd incorporates the Imprints of
Pen & Sword Aviation, Pen & Sword Maritime,
Pen & Sword Military, Wharncliffe Books, Pen and
Sword Select, Pen and Sword Military Classics and Leo
Cooper.

For a complete list of Pen & Sword titles please contact
PEN & SWORD BOOKS LIMITED
47 Church Street
Barnsley
South Yorkshire
S70 2AS, England
E-mail: enquiries@pen-and-sword.co.uk
Website: www.pen-and-sword.co.uk

Contents

Introduction   **1**

Chapter 1   A Poisonous Death
Jonas Mead and William Dazley,
Wrestlingworth, 1842   **4**

Chapter 2   God's Will
Charity Glenister, Heath & Reach, 1853   **15**

Chapter 3   A Deadly Argument
Jane Castle, Summeries Castle, 1859   **23**

Chapter 4   A Walk in the Dark
William Bradbury, Lilley, 1868   **33**

Chapter 5   A Scream in the Night
Sarah Marshall, Little Staunton, 1871   **41**

Chapter 6   The Body in the Bag
Lucy Lowe, Stagsden, 1876   **48**

Chapter 7   The Rage of a Silent Man
Effie Burgin, Bedford, 1895   **57**

Chapter 8   Too Drunk to Know
Harriet Reeve, Leighton Buzzard, 1915   **66**

Chapter 9   A Soldier's Tale
Amy Martin, Luton, 1915   **73**

Chapter 10   A Date With Death
Ellen Rault, Haynes Camp, 1919   **79**

Chapter 11   The Blunham Mystery
Mr & Mrs Marshall, Blunham, 1929   **90**

Chapter 12   A Sad Case of Insanity
Arthur Morley, Bedford, 1942   **98**

Chapter 13   The High Price of Fruit
Thomas Astle, Kempston, 1942   **103**

Chapter 14   The Body in the Sack Murder
Irene Manton, Luton, 1943   **109**

Chapter 15   A Moment of Madness
Phyllis Shields, Stotfield, 1960   **119**

Chapter 16   Tragedy on Deadman's Hill
The Hanratty Case, 1961   **122**

Index   **149**

Introduction

urder is a heinous crime. Yet it is also a crime that both fascinates and intrigues. Were that not the case then there would be no audience for the various television crime series that populate our TV channels. Our favourite fictional detectives would not exist and neither would their creators. But, of course, there is a recognised difference between the murder plots we watch on screen and those we read of in our daily newspapers. We readily accept the former for what it is, fiction, a contrived and often convoluted story line devised by a writer to tell a story. Often the murder or murders we witness are almost incidental to the development of the central character and his, or her, private life and the demons that share it. We suffer no personal sense of loss or suffer any collective grief as the stories unfold. Real life is very different.

Most murder is a contradiction in terms. On the one hand, it is an appalling act of violence that quite rightly elicits a damning response from all of us. On the other, it is a crime with a story to tell and it is the story that intrigues and fascinates. Who were those involved? Why did it take place? What were the consequences and what was the impact on those involved? These tend to be the questions we all ask and they do not change, even if the story is fictional. Human nature is such that we are born curious. We are enquirers in search of truth and, in the case of capital crime, that truth probably has more relevance than at any other time in history.

In the past, murder was considered by society as not only a heinous crime but also one that should carry the death penalty for anyone found to be guilty of it. That in turn meant the arena of the courtroom was a place of high drama. It was there that the characters involved gave their evidence, told their story and one by one cast their net about the prisoner in the dock. Unless, of course, defence counsel was of such calibre that it was able to rebut their claims and either discredit them or create doubt in the minds of the jurors over the veracity of the accounts they gave. Here was true theatre. From it come the real stories behind the facts. Those that tell of the characters involved, at whatever stage, in the events surrounding the crime and the motive. Herein lies our own fascination.

In his foreword to *Perfect Murder*, Colin Wilson writes: 'To understand the essence of a case it is not enough simply to know the gruesome details of the crime and of the police investigation. That produces merely the impression of the drama, and real life is always more subtle and complex than real drama.' He is right. Particularly when the death is either suspicious or remains unsolved. We need to know the details of those involved, the results of the inquest, the police investigation and the trial. Every case in a sense has its own peculiar atmosphere. No set of circumstances are ever really the same. The simple reason, of course, is human involvement.

The act of murder is the greatest of all crimes and is a very human one, caused in the main by a whole range of emotions, greed and jealousy, and our interest in it is a healthy one. We have a need to understand why another can be driven to take a life. We also have a very real fascination with the darker side of life and crimes of this nature perhaps cause us to pause and reflect on our own circumstances in relation to those we read about.

Foul Deeds & Suspicious Deaths Around Bedford is, therefore, an examination of those cases from the past that does just that. It's a collection of true stories recounting events that aroused similar passions amongst the local population and dominated newspaper headlines, not only across the county, but also in some cases countrywide. These cases also give an insight into social conditions prevalent at the time and how the law dealt with those involved; particularly when, unlike today, there was no DNA profile available, no ability to understand or interpret bloodstaining (until early in the nineteenth century), and post-mortems were, at best, rudimentary. For those involved, therefore, justice was a little ragged around the edges, but its search for the truth in its handling of each case unstinting.

In researching this book I never felt any person had suffered either ill treatment or inequity at the hands of the court. On the contrary, in the context of the time period of each case, I would say the law was applied well. But there is little doubt that along the journey I made, I met a number of characters I would have no wish to meet in real life.

I would like to take this opportunity of thanking those who have helped directly in the putting together of this book, and those whose work has contributed to the narrative. I am indebted to the staff of Bedfordshire and Luton Archives and Records Office, for whom nothing was ever too much trouble. The host of unnamed newspaper reporters whose dedication to detail has proven key to some of my research. Also, The *Bedfordshire Times, Details of Bedfordshire Murders 1840-2005, Bedfordshire Crime Statistics 1801-1878, Wikipedia, The Cowper and Newton Museum,* and *Hertfordshire & Bedfordshire Murders* by Paul Harrison. Every attempt has been made to contact owners of copyright for images used in this book where such exists. If any omission has been made it is not deliberate and no offence was intended.

CHAPTER 1

A Poisonous Death

The Murders of Jonas Mead and William Dazley
Wrestlingworth, 1842

For her, there was never such a thing as a failed marriage.

When Simeon Mead walked down the aisle with his new bride on a cold November day in 1835 he no doubt counted himself amongst the very fortunate; his bride, Sarah Reynolds, a tall, vivacious young woman of nineteen, had been hard won. A combination of looks and personality had ensured her place at the centre of village attention and there had been no lack of prospective suitors. But Sarah had never looked further than Simeon's door and the two had been lovers for over a year. Sister to three brothers and daughter to a father who had died in a debtors' prison eleven years earlier, meant her childhood had been far from easy. Marriage for Sarah, therefore, was no prelude to guaranteed happiness. She knew well enough the potential pitfalls and most probably understood better than most of her contemporaries just how demanding her commitment was going to be. But Sarah felt in Simeon she had found more than just a soul mate. Not that it mattered greatly, for if things went badly wrong she had already devised a plan. For her, there would never be such a thing as a failed marriage. All Simeon had to do was be good to her.

Initially, that was exactly what he was. Born into a farming community, Simeon would never be considered work-shy. Agriculture was what he knew and exactly where he intended to stay, so, when the prospect of unemployment loomed in early 1838, he moved the family home from Tadlow to Wrestlingworth. There, he took a job at New England farm and two years later Sarah gave birth to a son, Jonas. For both sides of the family the birth was auspicious; on the one hand it cemented the relationship and on the other it proved the

St Peter's church, Wrestlingworth where Jonas was baptised. The author

couple's fidelity. If any doubts had existed over the couple's continued compatibility they were banished at that moment. But Sarah was far from happy.

Toward the end of May 1840, six months after Jonas had been baptised in Wrestlingworth's parish church, Simeon took ill. At first it was thought he had suffered a bout of what could be termed gastric flu; his initial symptoms were simply pains in his stomach and a period of vomiting. But this slowly worsened. By early June he was unable to eat, his throat and mouth had swollen to such an extent he could only swallow with great effort and by the time of his death on 9 June this swelling prevented him from taking any liquids, and had affected much of his face and eyes.

For those that had known him as they gathered around his graveside a few days later, there was an undoubted sense of loss. Sarah, as the grieving widow, understandably received the villager's sympathy and the two families rallied round. In the circumstances she would have expected no less, nor was it unusual. There had been no attempt to explain the onset of Simeon's sudden illness or its cause. Medicine was still in its rudimentary stages. The notion of suspicious death was not one the authorities were keen to raise. Sarah was quick to move on. Four months after Simeon had been laid to rest, she was walking back down the aisle.

William Dazley was a twenty-one-year-old labourer. Just when the relationship had started is not known but Dazley was local, so it's reasonable to surmise they had been aware of each other for some time. Village gossip suggested that was a reasonable assumption though there appears to be little by the way of substantive evidence. Either way, they married on 11 October 1840 with no dissenting voice raised amongst the church's congregation. Tragically for young Jonas, it was not to be a marriage that would bring him any benefits. For him there was to be no succour in his time of need and only four weeks after the ceremony, he joined his father in the grave.

Sarah and William continued to live in Wrestlingworth but the marriage was far from successful. At times it was stormy, frequently contentious and some would say often combative, though there is nothing to support the notion that William was a violent husband. But Sarah had no plans to stay around long enough to find out if the disintegration of their relationship would turn him into one. On Sunday 23 October 1842, two years after their exchange of vows, William, like Simeon before him, fell ill.

Henry Sandal, the doctor at Potton, was brought to the house at a little after three o'clock that afternoon to treat his stomach pains and constant vomiting. He gave him carbonate of soda, diagnosed an irritation of the stomach and, not believing the condition to be serious, left. He was very wrong. By Tuesday, as the family gathered around his bedside, William's health was in terminal decline. Neighbour Mary Carver, concerned about the sudden deterioration suggested to Sarah that the two of them walk over to the doctor's house and ask him to call again. She agreed, but Dr Sandal was not about to leave his fireside. Instead, he sent the two back with an aperient powder (mild laxative) made up of tartrate of soda, powdered rhubarb and powdered ginger. This seemed to have some sort of recuperative effect and William rallied. So much so that when the doctor made an unexpected call at the house on the following day it was to find his patient showing clear signs of recovery. It was, however, a false dawn. By that same evening, William had once more lapsed. Unable to eat or drink because of a swollen throat, in constant pain and vomiting worse than at any other time, his condition had worsened severely. Desperate to find a way of alleviating his symptoms his mother, Elizabeth, who had been at the house since the onset of the illness, applied three leeches to his throat in an attempt to reduce the internal swelling – and a hot poultice was placed on his stomach. The poultice did little but the leeches, other than causing him to bleed profusely, did seem to help and, for a while, William rested. As he dozed she cleaned him up as best she could, and the vomit, which was contained in a bowl by the bed, she threw out into the neighbours' pig pen. On the following morning the neighbours' pig was dead. Two days later, so was William.

Alarm bells ought to have been ringing at that point, two husbands and one child dead in the space of two years, all three dying from similar symptoms. Certainly, Dr Sandel expressed surprise at his patient's unexpected death and requested that Sarah allow him to carry out a post-mortem. She refused, claiming it would be far too distressing for both her and William's immediate family. Without argument, he all too readily acceded, seemingly satisfied there had been nothing suspicious about the onset of William's illness or its devastating consequences, and returned to his surgery in Potton. But elsewhere, voices of suspicion were being raised amongst those that

Wrestlingworth village today. The author

did not share the doctor's views. Slowly, the rumour spread that William's death had been no act of God.

Whether Sarah was mindful of these misgivings, and the growing speculation in the village over her involvement in the three deaths, is doubtful. If she had been, surely she would have moved as far away from Wrestlingworth as she could. As it was, she stayed in the village, seemingly blissfully unaware and, within weeks of William's funeral, had even begun a relationship with local farm labourer, George Waldock, whom she had already chosen as her third husband. On 5 February 1843, their intended marriage was announced when banns were read in the parish church. But then her world came crashing down around her.

George Waldock had been involved throughout the previous year with another local woman. Jealous of the switch in his affections to the grieving widow, she went to see him and openly accused Sarah of triple murder. Waldock, who seems to have been one of the few that had never suspected Sarah of being so cunning, was horrified. He, in turn, stormed off to see his intended bride and withdrew his offer of marriage. In no uncertain terms he told Sarah she would have to prove her innocence before he could agree to marriage. Twenty-four hours later, he had the banns withdrawn and the wedding cancelled.

Gossip spread about the village like a virus and when it reached the door of Elizabeth Dazley, who had always harboured a suspicion over her son's death, she went hot foot to nearby Tadlow. There, she met with Simeon Mead's mother. Without preamble, she launched into an attack on her daughter-in-law, accused her of poisoning William and of doing exactly the same thing to both Simeon and his son, Jonas. It was the end for Sarah. An expanded and exaggerated version of that conversation found its way back to Wrestlingworth. In no time at all she had learned of it, and suddenly aware of the danger she was in, she packed up her belongings and made for London.

Within hours of her departure, Wrestlingworth's local policeman was knocking at the door of local magistrate Francis Pym, to pass on the rumour circulating around the village. Satisfied it was not without some substance, he, in turn, requested that Bedford's coroner, Ezra Eagles, issue an order to local police requiring them to exhume William Dazley's body and carry out a full autopsy on his remains.

On Monday 20 March 1843, he presided over the first stage

of the subsequent inquest, which was held at *The Chequers Inn*. William's body had already been disinterred and the coffin placed in the aisle of the parish church. There, in front of the coroner, prior to the opening of procedures, the lid had been removed and a formal identification carried out. As the court waited, Bedford surgeon Isaac Hurst, who had accepted the responsibility for carrying out the post-mortem, removed the whole of the alimentary canal from the throat to the intestine. This was placed and sealed inside a jar and despatched to the infirmary at Bedford for further examination. Back at the inn, the doctor then explained what was to happen during the examination of the body part he had taken and, after instructing police to arrest Sarah Dazley, the inquest was adjourned for five days.

Unknown to Sarah, after her arrival in the capital her brother, Edward Reynolds, who worked there as a tailor, wrote a letter. Concern over her sudden arrival at his house, and her unusual reticence when questioned as to why she had left the village, had disturbed him. So, in order to ascertain the reasons for her departure, the letter was sent to his elder brother in Potton. This found its way into the hands of local police and Sarah's fate was sealed. In London, City Police Inspector Woodroffe, alerted as to her whereabouts, made a formal arrest two days later.

On 23 March she stood in a London court and, after a legal argument over the city police's right to arrest her without a warrant, was released into the custody of Bedford police. Later that same day, she was brought by train to Biggleswade where she spent the night in a room at the *Spread Eagle Inn*. At ten o'clock the following day, she was brought into the inquest room at Wrestlingworth where the adjourned inquest was resumed. Hundreds of people attended, all desperate for a glimpse of the woman they believed to be a triple murderer.

Proceedings opened with evidence from George Hedley, a Bedford doctor, who had assisted Isaac Hurst to carry out a variety of tests on the organs removed from William Dazley's body. These tests, he explained, had taken more than forty-eight hours to complete but were conclusive and had provided irrefutable evidence of the presence of white arsenic. In pure form, a grey metal but usually seen as a powder in the form of arsenic trioxide. He told the hearing that it was odourless, tasteless and toxic to the gastrointestinal tract. In the case of William Dazley's death, he went on, the symptoms of his illness were fully consistent with it having been administered at some point and possibly in various quantities. Once ingested, it would have caused nausea, vomiting, abdominal pain and dry mouth, and the quantity found was sufficient to have killed him. This was the crucial evidence of the day and when the jury returned its verdict that Dazley had died from the effects of arsenic, it came as no surprise. Neither did the caveat that it had been administered, 'with a guilty knowledge by Sarah Dazley, his wife'.

Despite her protestations and vociferous denials, she was manacled and removed to Bedford Prison. There, she continued to insist there could be no charge to answer. She told Bedfordshire police that she had never given arsenic to William Dazley, either purposely or accidentally, and challenged them to prove otherwise. From her cell she continued to plead her innocence as she awaited her trial, refusing to acknowledge the weight of evidence against her, and that evidence was about to weigh even heavier.

On the 14 April, some three weeks after Sarah's imprisonment, Bedfordshire's coroner was told at a private meeting with the Reverend Twiss, rector of Wrestlingworth, that he ought to examine the deaths of Simeon and Jonas Mead. If Sarah had murdered one husband, so the argument ran, could she not have murdered two? From the rector's point of view it seemed certain she had. The circumstances surrounding the deaths, he told Ezra Eagles, were almost identical in every detail to those witnessed around the deathbed of William Dazley. Would it not be prudent, he urged, to exhume the bodies and examine them to be certain? It was a reasonable request. Almost everyone who had been in contact with Sarah had also heard of the continued speculation surrounding her past and coroner Eagles was no exception. He agreed with the rector and acceded to the request.

On 21 April, a coroner's court was reconvened at the *The Chequers*. Over the previous seven days a detailed examination had been carried out on the remains of the father and son. A far more difficult procedure than in the case of Dazley, simply because there was less body tissue to access as the two bodies had been in the ground some two and a half years. In the case of Simeon that meant little of the body remained, except the skeleton, and the results of the post-mortem were inconclusive. But with the remains of Jonas there was far more to work with and here, there was a major breakthrough. According to Dr Hedley, who had been involved with the Dazley case, the stomach still remained, as did the liver and bowels. From these

The Chequers Inn, *Wrestlingworth where the coroner's court was held.* The author

he was able to ascertain that the child had definitely consumed two or three grains of arsenic, more than enough to have caused his death. A second verdict of murder was returned and once more it named Sarah as the killer.

With two murders to choose from now there seemed little doubt of conviction. The dilemma was, which of the two to bring to court. The Crown chose the murder of Dazley as his was the most recent death, which meant there would be less likelihood of a successful challenge against the post-mortem results. It was felt that with a lapse of more than two years since young Jonas's death a good defence barrister may well have been able to pick holes in the prosecution case. Dazley's death on the other hand was still fresh in the public mind and the presence of arsenic irrefutable.

The trial itself opened at Bedford on Saturday 19 July 1843 before Baron Alderson. Sarah took her place in the dock and, in a voice racked by emotion, pleaded not guilty. Hundreds had turned out to witness the county's biggest trial to date and with space at a premium, every vantage point in the courtroom had been taken long before her arrival in court. After outlining the details of their case, the prosecution called Elizabeth Dazley, William's mother, as their first witness. Designed to set the scene for the rest of the day, she was skilfully taken through the last seven days of her son's life as she had witnessed them. From her place on the stand, before a hushed court, she recounted his symptoms, told how violent his illness was, how he constantly cried out for water, the colic like pains that gripped his stomach and terrible bouts of sickness that seemed to accompany his every waking hour. It was powerful, effective testimony. When she walked out of the room there could be no doubting the potency and dreadful efficiency of arsenic when consumed by the human body.

Dr Sandel followed up with details of the medicines he had prescribed or sold to Sarah, none of which contained arsenic. He described how he had seen William at the outset of his illness and midway through, and reiterated his surprise at the death. Defence counsel, a Mr O'Malley, challenged him over his failure to report the death to the coroner, arguing that had it appeared to be poisoning that caused the death, he should have recognised the symptoms. If, he went on, the man had been in such horrific circumstances throughout a whole week, ought the doctor to have not only noticed it but put a stop to what was alleged to have been taking place. It was an attempt to muddy the waters and a reasonable point to make. But Dr Sandel was not about to allow himself to be accused of mis-diagnosis. Arsenic poisoning, he told Mr O'Malley, was notoriously difficult to recognise. Its symptoms matched those of gastric fever, which was a common affliction and something over the years he had seen often. Unless he had stayed with his patient for every hour of every day, he would have seen nothing to suggest that he was witnessing a murder.

By the lunchtime break, these witnesses alone had damned Sarah Dazley. So effective had been their testimony that the defence counsel must have realised the hopelessness of their case. When, during the long afternoon that followed, a procession of witnesses offered up more and more evidence in support of the notion that their client was overwhelmingly guilty, there was nowhere for the defence team to go; particularly when two of the women that had been in the Dazley house at various times told the court that they had seen Sarah discard pills provided by the doctor and replace them with her own; this was damning, though almost certainly untrue. During his testimony, the doctor had listed the items given in his treatment of Sarah's husband and at no time had he given pills of any

The old prison on Bedford Bridge c1750. Author's collection

description. But it mattered little. The jury accepted the story and it was never refuted in court.

At the close of the day, it was left to Mr O'Malley to convince the jury members that what they had heard was nothing but flawed testimony. In his closing speech he argued strongly that it was flawed simply because it had been given not at the time of the death, but six months later. Memory, he insisted, was inevitably unreliable after such a lapse of time:

> *You have heard witnesses for the purpose of raking up every idle word and expression which the poor unfortunate woman had used, and which she had uttered months before the charge was brought against her . . .*

He attempted to show that, despite what appeared to be compelling evidence, there was no motive to the crime. Sarah Dazley, he told them, was in a stable marriage at the time of her husband's death. No witness had been produced to show that the marriage was either failing or had suffered because of violence by William. Then, pointedly, he asked them to consider where she had bought the arsenic if she had been responsible for committing murder. This latter point was probably the key to the whole trial. It is fair to say that no one had been produced to show just how the poison had been obtained as arsenic was a controlled poison and its purchases were logged. Sarah had, to all intents and purposes, only bought arsenic once and then only a pennyworth to deal with a rat infestation. It had been postulated in court that this purchase had been made a year earlier but no corroborative evidence was brought before the jury and no log detailing its sale had been found. So, for Mr O'Malley, it was a point he had to drive home and he certainly did his best. But there was no hope for his client. After an adjournment of thirty minutes she was declared guilty and sentenced to death.

On Saturday 5 August 1843, Sarah Dazley (nee Reynolds) appeared on the top of the gaol porch at twelve o'clock in the afternoon. A chaplain read prayers, while around her stood a group consisting of the prison governor, a surgeon and the executioner. The procession made its short walk to the foot of the ladder leading up to the scaffold. Once there she was asked if she had anything to confess. She said:

> *No, if I confess to the crime, I shall die with a lie in my mouth. I am innocent, and did not know when my husband died, that he had taken poison.*

She then ascended the ladder and was placed over the drop. There, her own hat was removed and replaced with a man's nightcap, which was pulled down over her head and face. The rope was then placed around her neck, secured to the beam above her and the bolts holding the trapdoor withdrawn. A crowd of somewhere in the region of 12,000 people gave a shriek as she fell to her death, then slowly drifted away back to their homes.

Chapter 2

God's Will

The Murder of Charity Glenister
Heath & Reach, 1853

Suddenly, bad tempered confrontation changed to murderous intent and Charity stood absolutely no chance.

bel Burrows was born in 1816 to parents who could ill afford to feed him and whose lives had been blighted by poverty since their marriage – an endemic amongst those forced to live, as they did, at the bottom end of society's social scale. It was caused, in part, by the life and death struggle with France, which had, over some twenty-five years, occasioned huge commercial losses to industry, and a government failure to implement much needed social reform. At the time of Napoleon's defeat at Waterloo, the price of bread was at its highest, wages at their lowest and the threat of revolution a very real danger. No law existed to enforce safety and safeguard sanitary conditions in the workplace, no local authority to provide drains for sewerage, no police force, no magistrates to enforce what law existed; and an act of parliament made it illegal for workers to form clubs, unions or friendly societies for fear these might become Jacobin.

Little wonder then that his childhood was to be as difficult as it was to be short. Abel had no real education throughout his growing years and, before he had become a teenager, was expected to contribute to the family income through work. He was classed as an adult by the time he was ten years old. It had a profound effect upon his mind. His mother's brother went mad and was locked away in a mental asylum by the time Abel had attained the age of twenty-five, and there were distinct signs that he was not to be far behind him.

At some time during the 1830s Abel had married and the couple had a daughter. But by this time he had already begun to exhibit a strange side to his character. At night, when seized by frequent bouts of insomnia, he would often rant and rage against God, waking the whole house up to quote scripture. Sometimes he even attacked those who managed to sleep. His mental decline was aided, in part, by his continued membership of the Primitive Methodist church, a religious order he had become involved with against the advice of his family, and whose evangelical message he earnestly believed.

By 1850, he had moved his family into a small house on the outskirts of Leighton Buzzard, at a place known as Heath and Reach; two hamlets forming a chapelry and lying between Leighton and Woburn. Reach, a small number of houses on a hill; Heath, made up of a similar number but occupying the lower, flatland below. The Burrows family house, close to that of his parents, was in Heath where he worked as a general labourer.

By this time his marriage had, not surprisingly, begun to falter. Frequent bouts of anger and his irrational behaviour had led to his wife fleeing the family home on more than one occasion, generally in the direction of his parents' house where she would be given a bed, usually that of her father-in-law, and shelter for the night. For her, it was more than just a safe haven.

Heath and Reach as it is today. The author

Abel's father, Francis, who had grown accustomed to his son's unpredictable nature over the years, had become the peacemaker. To him fell the task of arbitration and he accepted his role readily enough. Usually a couple of hours were sufficient, though sometimes it would take all night. So, when he was awakened around midnight on Friday 25 November 1853, by his daughter-in-law hammering on the front door, it was nothing out of the ordinary.

Over the years Francis had taught himself to accept the frequent interruptions to his sleep. He may even have developed the art of being a light sleeper, which was a necessity where his son was concerned and no doubt a practice that generally ensured minimum disruption in his own house. As had become his common practice, he left his wife asleep and went downstairs to let her in. After listening to the familiar rant of a disaffected wife, he sorted her out a bed for the night, then walked the short distance to his son's home. The two men stayed up talking until three in the morning by which time Abel, exhausted by the constant arguing, had fallen asleep. Satisfied there was nothing else he need do, Francis left him alone and returned to his own kitchen to make tea.

Unable to sleep, he dozed in a chair beside the fire until a little after six o'clock in the morning when the house began to stir. Seventy-six-year-old Charity Glenister was the first to rise. No relative of the family, she had been taken in by them two years earlier and paid her way by doing odd jobs about the house and around the village. Everyone knew her and Francis liked having her around the place. She was a good cook and company for his wife. For Charity, finding the Burrows family when she did had been a godsend and had put a roof over her head when she most needed it. Only Abel resented her place in the household. Though he never explained why, his disapproval at her presence had always been obvious from his manner alone, which had always been hostile. Not that they argued, far from it, Abel saved his temper for his wife. Instead, he was simply brusque and discourteous whenever the two met. Leastways, that had been the case up until that morning.

When he walked into the kitchen just after 8 am looking for his wife and something to eat, this ill-mannered approach to Charity had been replaced with a sort of resentful anger. Chastened over the previous night's marital fallout and desperate to allocate blame, he had spent the early hours of the morning searching his mind for an external cause. Before he had left his own home to walk the short distance to his father's house, that cause, he had decided, was the evil Charity. The logic may have been warped, but to Abel it made perfect sense. To him, relations with his wife had deteriorated significantly since the old woman's arrival at his parents. In turn, every argument with his wife had driven her to seek refuge with his father, where, in receipt of what she considered sage advice from the old woman, his wife had returned home ever more belligerent than when she had left – fuelled, he believed, by Charity's hatred of himself and her criticism of his mental state. It was complete nonsense, of course, but to Abel it was the absolute truth and he intended to do something about it. Neither spoke when they met in the kitchen and within minutes of his arrival at the house, Charity, eager to be away, had left. Whether she suspected that Abel's mental make up had taken a severe battering over night is not known. Perhaps something in his demeanour posed more of a threat than normal. Either way, her departure from the house was sudden. So was Abel's. He wanted his moment, his confrontation, but once outside something inside snapped. Suddenly, bad tempered confrontation changed to murderous intent and Charity stood absolutely no chance.

Francis Burrows had worked for years as a road labourer. Each day he spent his hours either digging or smashing rocks to form the stone for road-laying. The tools of his trade, a wheelbarrow and a heavy sledgehammer, he stored in a nearby barn. Abel wanted the hammer. Almost without thinking, he made straight for the barn, seized the hammer, then went straight for Charity. She saw him coming and knew the hammer was meant for her. In a desperate attempt to escape, she ran for the nearest house, next door neighbours the Adams family. There, alerted by her screams, Sarah Adams, who thought the old woman was simply hammering at the door to tell them Abel was about to attack his own mother, let her in. From across the street Abel never broke his stride. At that point Sarah suddenly realised it was Charity he was after and quickly forced the door shut again and threw the bolts. It made no difference to Abel's relentless progress. Without speaking, he simply smashed his way into the Adams' house, pushed Charity to the floor and hit her once across the back of the head with the hammer. As she lay stunned on the floor he paused, lifted it again and then continued to hit her until she was dead. At that point, Thomas Adams, who had been awoken by all the commotion, ran downstairs and attempted to disarm him. It was a futile attempt and almost cost him his life. Abel was far too strong and, after a

CHAPTER 3

A Deadly Argument

The Murder of Jane Castle
Summeries Castle, 1859

What he found stayed with him for the rest of his life.

Summeries Castle, a mile or so south of Luton, is today as it has been for years, a picturesque spot, a place for picnics and lazy days. From its position on top of a hill, the castle has a commanding view of the immediate countryside around, as it was intended to do by its builders, and the steepness of the hillside give it a decisive advantage over any would-be attackers. At some point in the late eighteenth and early nineteenth centuries gravel or chalk was extracted from land at the base of the hill. These outcrops have left behind a small mound beside a shallow pit, now much overgrown, but once a favoured site for couples in search of privacy. Known locally as 'the dell', it was once also the place of a particularly brutal and bloody murder.

At around half-past eleven on the morning of 9 August 1859, ostler (horsekeeper) John Purser was returning to Model Farm, which sat just beyond the castle site, with a cart-load of coal. As the narrow track skirted the base of the castle mound, he noticed to his right what he initially took to be a woman's dress. Stopping the horse, he jumped down onto the road to make a closer inspection. What he found stayed with him for the rest of his life.

The body he stumbled across was that of a woman. She lay on her back with her legs beneath her as if she had fallen backwards from a kneeling position. Her throat had been cut and there was an immense quantity of blood where the body was lying; she was still quite warm and blood still oozed from a gaping neck wound. The woman's shawl and bonnet lay some two metres away, both marked by bloodstaining and a blood trail ran from her position at the centre of the dell to the road behind where the cart had stopped. As the ostler followed the

The rutted track leading toward Summeries Castle, which has no public access today. The author

blood spots he could clearly see signs of a scuffle by the road-side, footprints had broken up the roads dusty surface and a little distance further on was another pool of dried blood. At that point he made for Luton and the nearest police house.

An hour later, Luton Police Superintendent, Samuel Pope, arrived at the scene. In a thorough examination of the murder site he was quickly able to ascertain that the initial attack had definitely taken place on the road where the ostler had found blood. But a second blood trail indicated that the victim had not been killed at that point but had escaped her attacker and run off in the direction of the castle. This trail, some 125 metres long, led him to another pool of blood beside a stile that led to the castle mound, before finally taking him into the centre of the dell where she had died. To the Superintendent, all this implied that the final and most brutal part of the murder had been where the body finally came to rest. There, he deduced, in the middle of the overgrown pit, dying from horrific injuries, she had been forced to her knees and put to death. At that juncture, as far as Superintendent Pope was concerned, there had been less of a murder and more of an execution and he was determined to find the man responsible.

Whilst all this was going on, PC John Bennett at Welwyn was opening his front door to a man he thought he knew very well. Joseph Castle, a twenty-nine-year-old out-of-work maltsman, had crossed his path on more than one occasion. Though his offences had never been serious, Bennett had always cast a watchful eye in his direction. When he saw him on his doorstep, something told him that what was staring back at him was a guilty conscience. He invited the man in and made him tea. As the two sat drinking across the dinner table, Castle told the policeman he had rowed with his wife. The argument, he told Bennett, had been serious, very serious and it had been violent. But, he insisted, he had no idea what had become of her and he had not harmed her. It was a strange thing to say and the constable quite rightly became suspicious of Castle's motives for making the house call. He knew there was more to it. People rarely called to the police house unless there was an offence to report. Experience had taught him to be wary. The more he looked at the man on the opposite side of the table the more he saw. Castle was dishevelled, tired, dirty and, more importantly, as he leaned back in his chair he exposed a spattering of small bloodstains across the front of his clothing. It was enough for Bennett. Reaching across the table, he took the teacup from the man's hand and told him candidly that he believed he had done something to his wife. Castle, of course, loudly protested his innocence. It made no impression on the policeman. Better men than he had taken exception to his forthright approach and all had been proven liars, so he was not about to take any chances and Castle was arrested.

Two hours later, PC Bennett arrived in Luton. There he acquainted the Superintendent with Castle's story. Both men agreed it appeared likely the body that had been removed to the *Heron Inn* was that of Castle's wife, Jane. A formal identification by her family later that night confirmed it, and Castle was formally charged with murder just after midnight. On the following day, he was brought to Bedford and incarcerated in prison.

Over the following weeks it transpired that the Castle's marriage had been far from happy. According to those that knew the couple there had been cracks in the relationship even before they had taken their vows, in the main caused by Castle's irrational jealousy. His behaviour toward Jane almost from the moment the couple had left the church had been at best objectionable, at worst offensive. Believing her incapable of being faithful, he had refused to allow her to work or associate with friends and neighbours. But even that was not enough. A word or a smile would send him wild with anger if it were not directed solely at himself. Leaving the house alone would precipitate a rage that could last for days and receiving visitors, particularly male, was a cue for violence. Tired of her fidelity being constantly questioned and scrutinised, she had attempted to leave him some months earlier. It ended in dismal failure after he had discovered her plan and, in order to thwart any future designs she may have harboured, he had torn up all her clothes. But Jane was not to be denied. Earlier in the year, the couple had moved to Castle's uncle's house, in Ware. There Jane had conspired with the uncle's daughter to set a date by which she could escape back to Luton.

Details of why she had chosen 8 August and the circumstances surrounding her death slowly emerged as the year progressed. By winter 1859, enough information had been gathered to enable police, with some degree of certainty, to begin to piece together the story of Jane's last few days and the circumstances surrounding her horrific death.

It appeared that the date had been chosen simply because the

The Town Hall, Luton, c1900. Author's collection

two women knew Castle would be away from home during the day. Also, with most of her clothes destroyed, her load would be light to carry. Paying for carriage was never likely to figure. Jane only had three pence in her purse when she was found. But she was young, fit, and the weather was good, important in light of the fact that the journey was some twenty-one miles. Unfortunately, she was also naïve.

At six o'clock that same night, some nine or ten hours after she had left Ware, Castle discovered her absence. Initially uncertain as to where she had gone, he first went to Hatfield railway station to check if anyone had seen her board a train. From there he walked to Cromer Hyde, some thirteen miles from Ware, to the house of Esther Archer, the woman who had taught Jane as a child and someone he knew she trusted. She refused to allow him into her house and the two exchanged words out on the street. But in her anger the retired schoolmistress let slip that she had seen Jane earlier in the day. A neighbour, disturbed by all the commotion, then added that she had gone back to her parent's house in Luton. That was all he needed to know. At just after ten o'clock that same night, as Jane ought to have expected, he arrived outside the house on York Street.

There were no lights burning as he approached and initially he believed everyone had gone to bed. Not wanting a confrontation with Jane's father, Francis Whitworth, in the dark, he therefore decided his first priority was to find somewhere to sleep. There he was lucky. He knew that his father-in-law had a plait dye-house just across the street. More importantly he guessed it would have been left unlocked. It seemed sensible to make use of it and stay out of sight until dawn. Then, just as he began to make his way across the street, he caught a glimpse of a woman. From her size and silhouette it had to be Jane. Without waiting, he dashed back, grabbed a hold of her and pushed her back against a wall. She screamed. The voice was not hers; he panicked, let go of her and ran. For the next two hours he prowled about Luton in search of somewhere else to get his head down for the night. At just after midnight, after a fruitless two hours and a brief brush with the police, he decided to return. It seemed ridiculous not to. The dye-house was perfect for his needs and only a stones throw from where he needed to be in the morning. Besides which, he told himself, he would already be in a cell if the woman had made any sort of formal complaint.

At 7 next morning, he calmly lifted the latch of the

York Street, Luton as it looks today. The author

Whitworth's door and walked into the house. Jane's sister, Emily, was making tea. Without any preamble he asked her if her father was still at home and whether it was true that Jane had returned there the previous day. A startled Emily, who had always disliked Castle but had never been afraid of him, expressed no surprise at his sudden arrival and readily told him Francis had gone out, adding disdainfully that her sister was upstairs sleeping in her mother's bed. After a short pause, he asked her if she would have any objection to him going up to see her. In no position to object, despite her reservations, Emily hesitated for a moment then reluctantly stepped aside to let him pass.

Castle found her wide awake and sitting up. Feigning tiredness, he told her he needed to sleep and without waiting for an invitation pulled off his boots and climbed in beside her. Unable to stop him and angry that he had followed her she rolled away, turned her back on him and refused to speak. But to Castle that was a familiar, probably even expected reaction and he ignored it. Talking to the back of her head, he told her she had to return home with him, that she was to forget the past and in return he would change his ways, become a new man.

But Jane had heard it all before. To her it was a familiar story. A plea for forgiveness and reconciliation that had become all too familiar over the last two years and one she was no longer prepared to countenance. As she lay there mute, she knew there was to be no going back. This time, for her, the separation was permanent.

Concerned over Castle's protracted stay in the bedroom, Emily called up for her sister to go downstairs to breakfast. The call was timely and probably the cue Jane had been waiting for. Without acknowledging her sister and despite Castle's attempt to stop her, she hauled herself out of the bed and went downstairs. There she was joined by her other sister, Ellen. In muted tones, the three women discussed what was to become of her, much to the annoyance of Castle, who for the next two hours strained to hear what was taking place on the floor below, finally forcing him to give up his protest at 9 am out of sheer frustration.

When he eventually joined Jane in the kitchen it was to find breakfast over, leastways for him. So, ignored by the sisters, he sat by the fire until ten o'clock, smoking his pipe. At which point Jane broke her silence and told him to leave. He, as she must have expected, refused. The two argued and, eventually, in order to placate him, she offered to walk part of the way back to Ware with him if he would agree to go. Castle, after some persuasion, finally gave in and they eventually left the house together. At that point it appeared Jane believed she was finally going to be set free.

But Castle, of course, had never intended that his wife be freed from their failing marriage. When he had arrived in Luton he had only one objective in mind, to stop her at all costs. In his mind she was never to be allowed to destroy their relationship and to that end he had arrived armed and prepared to kill. When the two of them set out on the road to Summeries Castle it was to be the last walk she would ever take.

Though by the time of his trial, on 14 March 1860, before Mr Justice Williams, the details concerning Castle's involvement in her death were still somewhat vague. Throughout his incarceration in Bedford Prison, although he had made a statement regarding everything that had happened up until the killing, he had steadfastly refused to implicate himself in her murder. In fact he denied there had been a murder, claiming instead that Jane must have committed suicide. This, despite the evidence of blood on his clothing and the discovery of the knife that did the damage found lying twenty metres from the body. When he took his place in the dock before a packed courtroom, he pleaded not guilty and appeared confident in his innocence. Six months behind bars had done little it appeared to shake his self-belief. Without doubt it was a sham. One thing Joseph Castle was not, was delusional; he had adequately demonstrated that to the doctors who assessed his mental capability in the run up to the trial. More likely, he felt after his initial statement that had he no choice, despite the evidence against him. If he had retracted his claim of suicide before the court convened he would have forced his counsel to argue insanity, which he probably knew would carry absolutely no weight with the jury. Apparent sheer bravado was what led the reporter of the *Bedford Times* to tell his readers that:

> *He neither appeared to have the slightest notion of the awful position in which he stood, nor of the awful consequences of his guilt. The past, the present, and the future seemed to him to be matters of total indifference . . .*

Whether or not that is true he must have known once the results of the post-mortem were delivered to the jury that the case was as good as over, and so it proved.

Surgeon Patrick Benson took the stand toward the end of the morning. He told the court that Jane Castle had sustained two distinct wounds. One had been inflicted as a cut across the throat, which would not have killed her. The second was a stab wound, again to the throat, but deep into the neck severing the windpipe. Significant, because whilst the initial wound was not necessarily life threatening it had caused her to lose a deal of blood, so much, he insisted, that it would have rendered her unable to inflict the second and more deadly wound:

> *In consequence of the loss of blood caused by the first wound, the exhaustion would have been so great as to have rendered her inca-pable of inflicting the second . . . The force required would have been considerable . . .*

He also found cuts to her fingers, which appeared to confirm that there had been a struggle. At some point in the attack, according to his testimony, Jane had attempted to defend herself. Furthermore, he told the judge, the murder had most probably not taken place on the road but in the dell itself. From the evidence available and an examination of the site his opinion was that she had actually been killed where she had been found:

My opinion is that the position of the body when found was made by force. On examining where her legs were, which I at first did not see, I found that her knees protruded, her legs were bent back, so that her thighs rested upon the heels and the calves of the legs. My opinion is that she went on her knees, or was forced on them, and in that position she was forced backward. From the observation I made at the time, my opinion is that the wound causing her death was inflicted in the dell where she lay . . .

When the doctor stepped down from the stand, for Castle the case was over. Suicide as a motive had been utterly discredited, as had his insistence that she had been alone, cuts to her fingers obviously proved otherwise. Add to that the fact that he had blood on his clothes, the knife had been his, and the two of them had left the house in Luton together, and it rapidly became clear the evidence against him was simply overwhelming. The parade of witnesses that followed on from the doctor's testimony merely helped tie the noose tighter.

The Barrister, Mr Mills, who had defended Castle stoically throughout the day, made a valiant attempt in his closing speech to sway the jury toward a manslaughter verdict. The final wound, he argued, had not been intended to have been so deadly but inflicted in the heat of the moment. It was a point lost on the jurors. They returned a guilty verdict and Castle was sentenced to death.

On Friday 6 April, twenty-four hours before his execution, he finally confessed. After a visit from his mother and brother, during which he continued to deny his involvement, he asked to see the prison governor. In a lengthy and moving interview, which the governor recorded, he explained his reasons and then described in detail just what had taken place near Summeries Castle:

. . . The murder did not take place in the dell hole. It was done on the side of the road where the struggles were said to have taken place. I done it with my left hand. A short interval elapsed after I gave her the first wound; it was done from here to here (he passed his fingers from his ear to his throat). As soon as she found she was wounded she said, "I'll punish you." She was standing up at the time I did it. I seized hold of her the second time and entered the knife under her ear, and thrust it in the direction of the windpipe. As soon as she had received the second wound she said, "Joe, you have done it at last!" . . . She walked toward the dell hole, and she there tumbled in; she was not dragged. I saw her

in the dell hole on her knees in the attitude of prayer, with both hands lifted up toward heaven. When I left her she was alive . . .

Later that same day he wrote a letter detailing his life, his relationships and his feelings for the woman he had murdered. In it he expressed his regret at having murdered her and his wish that life could have led him to a better end. It is a sad, reflective document and marked his final farewell.

He was executed in front of the county prison at midday the following day.

CHAPTER 4

A Walk In The Dark

The Murder of William Bradbury Lilley, 1868

Worsley's reaction was both instant and violent.

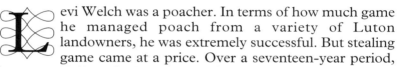

evi Welch was a poacher. In terms of how much game he managed poach from a variety of Luton landowners, he was extremely successful. But stealing game came at a price. Over a seventeen-year period, between 1851 and 1868, he was imprisoned on no less than eleven occasions. Mostly the sentences were short, three or four months on average, though in some cases only a matter of weeks. His longest sentence was fifteen months, served after being caught by gamekeepers carrying a weapon on a night poaching expedition. This longer sentence and the circumstances surrounding it, is what added significantly to his reputation as a hard man. Poaching to Levi Welch, it seems, was not a necessity more a way of life and violence merely a consequence. Known across much of Bedfordshire by those whose job it was to stop his nocturnal activities, his presence around the various villages, therefore, rarely went unnoticed. Generally it precipitated an increased level of security amongst local farmers and their gamekeeping teams.

By the summer of 1867, yet again a wanted man, he was in Luton with two other poachers: William Worsley, who had worked with him on numerous occasions in the past, and James Day, a comparative novice with almost no poaching experience. On 3 August, after making a potential sale in a pub to a local butcher for half a dozen game birds, the group had decided to raid a farm on the outskirts of the small village of Lilley. To that end they had all met in the *Royal Oak,* Round Green, which gave them easy access to the Hitchin road, at around nine o'clock that night. For the next three hours, all three drank heavily. Keeping a clear head was obviously not part of Welch's plan. He knew the layout of the land around

Hitchin Road, Round Green as it looks today. The author

and had intended that the birds were not to be taken until around dawn. Gamekeepers were usually scarce at that hour of the day. Until then, he had planned that the three sleep in barns at Whitehill farm, which lay about a mile from Lilley. When the landlord called time at just before midnight that's exactly where all three intended to go. Had it not been for the amount of alcohol they had all consumed, the night would probably have gone off exactly as planned. But drink affects different people in different way, and of the three men it was Worsley that felt its impact more keenly than his friends.

Seemingly energised by the beer, the minute they all stepped out onto the street he took the lead and disappeared into the darkness. Day, trailing at the back, shouted out after some fifty metres that he had lost sixpence and was going back to the pub to fetch a match. Welch ignored him and went off after Worsley who he could no longer see. Then came a shout from ahead of him that a man was lying dead in the road. The voice was Worsley's and when Welch finally found him he was stooping over the body of William Bradberry. He could be certain of the identity despite the darkness because Bradberry was a man they both knew. Unsure about what to do next, Welch then turned the body onto its back. At which point Worsley told him to search the pockets. Never squeamish around death and ever eager to take advantage of any opportunity to profit, Welch needed no second invitation. Pulling a knife from his own jacket, he systematically cut away all the pockets he could find whilst Worsley made a quick search of the ground around. Net result of the robbery was four shillings and sixpence (22½p) and two brown paper parcels. But Bradberry was not dead. He moaned as Welch manhandled him. Worsley's reaction was both instant and violent. He deliberately kicked the dying man at the base of the skull then stooped down, lifted his head and smashed it back onto the road beneath. Welch realised at that juncture that Bradberry had met with no accident. But there was no time to debate the point. James Day was running up the road toward them after his fruitless search for his sixpence. Behind him they could both hear other voices all alerted by Worsley's initial shout.

Bradberry was carried from the road to the *Jolly Topers* public house. All three poachers assisted. In fact it was Welch that fetched water to wash the blood from the man's face – though not out of concern, more out of duty. A doctor arrived some half an hour later and Bradberry died shortly afterwards, without ever regaining consciousness. The poachers slowly made their way to the barns at Whitehill farm.

The Jolly Topers *public house where the body was taken after the murder.* The author

The narrow track that leads to Whitehill Farm, today much as it was in 1868. The author

During the night, as Day slept, Worsley told Levi Welch that he had hidden the two parcels in the hedgerow. One of them, he said, contained a new pair of trousers and if Levi would take the money he would keep the trousers. Welch agreed. He then pulled out a short metal winch from his pocket, the type used to open and close a kitchen range (a necessary tool in a Victorian kitchen), and told Welch he had used it to hit Bradberry, adding that it belonged to his sister, Mary Ann. Welch was horrified, not at the murder but at Worsley's failure to throw the weapon away. In a heated exchange, out of earshot of Day, he told him it would incriminate them both and had to go. So, realising Welch was right, Worsley agreed to return it without her knowledge later that day. That satisfied him and the two men slept until around 5 am.

Curious as to what had happened in Round Green after they had left, it was then agreed to abandon their plans and return. On the way Day found the sixpence he had lost during the night and whilst he was distracted Welch threw away the knife he had used to cut out Bradberry's pockets. At that point they met Worsley's wife who told them police were in the village and perhaps it would be prudent to go no further, though her concern had more to do with their poaching activities than murder. Welch thought the advice worth heeding so all three split up and went off their separate ways. Over the next few days all three were interviewed by police as a matter of course, but by 20 August it became clear to all that they had become suspects. By that time, Luton surgeon, Kit Tomson had completed and published the results of his post-mortem. On that report he had stated categorically that Bradberry had been murdered. All witnesses were re-interviewed. From those interviews police then pieced together everyone's movements on the night of the killing – a painfully slow process, but bit by bit they began to realise that only Welch and Worsley could have carried out the attack. Two days later, along with Day, they were arrested. All three denied having any involvement.

On 24 August, Worsley then made the first of three statements in which he accused Levi Welch of being the killer. In all of them he stated that he had no idea Bradberry had been murdered until the following morning when Welch had confessed. Up until that point, he told police, he did not even know that anything had been stolen from the dead man. What had been taken, he told Superintendent Pope, had all been hidden in the hedgerows near to the murder site and was still there. This was borne out by a later search that recovered everything except the four shillings and sixpence.

When Welch heard what Worsley had done he was incensed and made his own statement. At odds with Worsley's, it obviously gave a different account of events but – without any apparent substantive evidence to support it – police decided his account was more truthful. Welch was then offered a reduced charge if he would agree to take the witness stand and tell his story to a jury. He had no hesitation.

The trial opened before Judge Baron Bramwell on 23 March 1868. It was essentially a forgone conclusion. With Levi Welch's testimony there was to be no going back for Worsley, though defence counsel made a valiant effort. Their stance from the outset was that Welch was a liar and that it had been he that struck the fatal blows. Mr Metcalfe, who represented Worsley, did his best to sow the seeds of doubt in the jurors' minds. Reminding them that the night was dark, no lamps lit the road, only Welch and Worsley were present when the attack had taken place, and no one else saw the blows that struck down William Bradberry. In a lengthy speech to the jury at the

THE LUTON MURDER.

THE EXECUTION

OF WORSLEY.

TUESDAY MORNING, MARCH 31.

We have already published, and commented upon, the memorial sent up from this town to the Home Office for a commutation of the capital sentence on Worsley, the man convicted of the recent murder near Luton. In due course that memorial was received and fully considered, and the Secretary of State referred the matter to Baron Bramwell, whose unqualified approval of the justice of the verdict decided the Home Secretary to allow the law to take its course. Colonel Gilpin, M.P., in deference to the wishes of a large body of his constituents, had a private interview with the Secretary of State, as Mr. Hardy had declined to receive a deputation in reference to the presentation of a memorial, but the Home Secretary stated that in consequence of a communication he had received from the Judge he could hold out no hopes of a reprieve. Col. Stuart, M.P., also interested himself in the matter, but the Secretary of State remained inflexible. The final decision of the Home Office, conveyed in the following letter, was received by Mr. Roberts, Governor of the Gaol, at a late hour on Saturday evening, through the kindness of the Postmaster, the letter not being deliverable in the ordinary course till Sunday morning.

"Whitehall, 28th March, 1868.

"Sir,—I am directed by Mr. Secretary Hardy to acquaint you that, having fully considered the case of William Worsley, in whose behalf you applied to him, he regrets that he can see no grounds to justify him in advising her Majesty to interfere with the due course of law.

"I am, Sir, &c.,

"A. F. O. LIDDELL.

"Rev. B. Backhouse, Bedford."

Before the arrival of this letter the promoters of the memorial had been informed that one of the jurors on Worsley's trial was disqualified by reason of deafness. This statement was made on the 26th March, and seemed to be reliable. The result of a personal interview with the juryman referred to dissipated, however, what slight hope had sprung up from this source: and this disappointment, supplemented by the intelligence conveyed in the foregoing letter, cut away every ground of hope for the respite of the unfortunate convict.

Similar efforts at Luton met with precisely the same termination. On the evening of Friday, the 27th of March, a town's meeting was held there, Mr. E. Lucas in the chair, and a resolution adopted in favour of the commutation of the capital sentence, on the motion of the Rev. Thos. Hands, seconded by the Rev. T. R. Stevenson. The resolution was unanimously adopted by an immense meeting, and on the motion of Mr. Wm. Willis, seconded by the Rev. T. J. Lee (vicar of Christ's church), was forwarded to the Home Secretary. A

The convict made several statements, which were taken down by the Governor and also attested by himself and the Chaplain. These will be found below. In one of these statements he confessed his guilt. He also wrote a last letter to his friends, which we publish. Up to the last moment he was most desirous that this letter should be sent to his friends. In fact before going to the scaffold he requested the Governor, in the presence of the Chaplain, that the contents of the letter should be made known to the public, and he hoped, as his last words, that the public would profit from the lesson which was to be learnt from his miserable doom.

From the time the Chaplain visited the convict, till the procession was formed to the scaffold, Worsley remained assiduous in prayer and seemed deeply sensible of the awful nature of the ordeal through which he had so soon to pass.

During a recent visit of his friends they suggested to him whether he would not desire to be attended by any other minister, but he refused, and stated over and over again that he was perfectly satisfied with the attentive and earnest ministrations of the Chaplain of the prison.

Worsley did not receive the Sacrament, nor did he make any request to that effect. He was entered on the Gaol register as a member of the Church of England.

Shortly before eight o'clock, the hour appointed for the execution, the under sheriff (T. Hooper, Esq., of Biggleswade), was introduced to the convict on the landing outside the condemned cell, the same cell, we may state, as that in which the murderer Castles had been detained pending his execution eight years ago.

Just outside the door of this cell the chapel door opens from the vestibule or landing, and it was at a short distance from the chapel door that the operation of pinioning took place.

Calcraft, who arrived in Bedford on Monday evening, here pinioned the convict's arms, whilst the man sat upon a low stool. Worsley made no resistance whatever, and asked the Governor of the Gaol to accompany him to the scaffold.

The process of pinioning over, the procession started at about five minutes to eight o'clock. Two warders led the way, whilst the prison bell tolled slowly and dismally to announce the culprit's doom.

The Chaplain came next in order wearing a surplice over his academical gown; next came the unfortunate convict, pale and haggard, but firm in step and strong in nerve, his mind being evidently braced to meet the last penalty of the law. On his right hand walked the Governor, on his left Calcraft, the executioner. The officers of the prison brought up the rear.

The procession moved slowly along the main corridor of the prison, out to the porter's lodge, and up a flight of steps in this lodge to the roof, on which the gallows had been erected on Monday, draped with sable cloth to a considerable height all round. Worsley was clad in the dress he wore at the trial.

As the procession passed the room in the vestibule in which the reporters were assembled, the convict turned towards the representatives of the press, and lifting

I cannot tell v ral people ask out that night coming back 1 met Day and drunk or had 1 at the Jolly T the doctor, W drunk and a 1 knocked down the big winch pocket on the back to my sis morning, and afterwards, co Welch if he hi ning of the we find it. I neve of the robbery Bradberry. 'T Sunday mornin o'clock. I was t robbed and his morning if he h He said, ' Yes, to have done i had put the th am called Fran well for you,' look well wear things. I neve the magistrates Welch has swo I suffer for it I must have had it else he would brother Obadia affair and what berry. I told Welch had hit I being robbed, into and got up I should be br study over it as such a case, 'I irelsome or fight have had reasoi quarrelsome, '

" (Signed)

" (Countersign " RO

The following i of the Governor,

SECOND S

" Condem

" The following ley is in his own take down in wri " I have just tell you. It was the man spoke o

How the Bedford Times *reported the murder in March 1868. The* Bedford Times

end of the trial he made reference to Levi Welch's criminal record and what he believed to be his inability to tell the truth:

He [Welch] *has put himself forward in such an unblushing way, he has admitted himself the perpetrator of many crimes of almost unparalleled enormity, that I have no hesitation in charging him deliberately with the commission of this crime. These two men came out of the public house together and Welch went on in advance . . . It is clear that Welch did steal all those things. It is clear that he did tell Worsley he had stolen them, and where he had placed them; it is manifest that Worsley did not go with him to hide them. Worsley gives the police the account he receives from Welch, and the police find everything in the places pointed out . . . Welch robbed the man; and gentlemen, the man who robs a man has a strong motive for reducing him to a state in which he could be robbed with impunity, and what robber would be more likely to reduce his victim to that state . . . than this man Welch . . .*

So it went on. It was a powerful argument and one the judge appeared to have great sympathy with. He, too, seemed to have doubts over Welch's testimony and told the jury that they must treat it with due caution:

He had been repeatedly convicted . . . He robs that man on that night whilst the man lies bleeding on the road and in his last gasp . . . He has confessed to violence; he has confessed to perjury; he

The village of Lilley. The author

has admitted he robbed this bleeding man who was in fact a corpse. You have had the unspeakable advantage of hearing and seeing him, and must judge whether you can extract a portion of truth out of the evidence he lays before you . . .

It made no difference, after a twenty minute adjournment they returned a verdict of guilty and Worsley was sentenced to death.

The *Bedford Times & Bedford Independent* certainly believed Worsley to be innocent and in their columns supported all efforts to commute the sentence to life. On Tuesday 31 March they even published Welch's criminal record in an attempt to show that he had lied. But of course they were wrong and hours before his public execution William Worsley signed a full confession. In it he admitted that he had lied about Welch and had continued to lie ever since simply because he thought it would earn a reprieve:

. . . I meant telling all along when I saw there was no reprieve, although many won't believe what I say . . . I never knew that the blow struck Bradberry when I struck him . . . I never saw Welch after leaving the public house until after I had struck Bradberry . . .

One hour later Worsley was met by his executioner, Calcraft, and taken up a short flight of stairs onto the roof of the porter's lodge, where the scaffold had been erected, and was executed as the prison clock struck 8 am.

CHAPTER 5

A Scream in The Night

The Murder of Sarah Marshall
Little Staunton, 1871

Sarah Marshall's body lay dead across the bed, her feet hanging over the end . . .

Born in 1819, Sarah Marshall had spent much of her life living in or around the small village of Little Staunton on the northern edge of the county border. At some point in her life she had been a schoolteacher but by the late 1840s had suffered a significant mental decline. Diagnosed, in the parlance of the day, as having lunatic tendencies but not considered dangerous to others, she was never certified insane and allowed to remain within her community. Kimbolton doctor, Joseph Hemming, was given the task of watching over her health when he became local surgeon in 1850 and ensuring, as much as it was possible to do, that her mental state remained constant. The task was in no way an onerous one. Old Sally, as she was known locally, really required very little by way of medical intervention. Well capable of looking after herself in all respects when she chose to, meant that Dr Hemming's role was more a simple watching brief. But Sarah was most certainly a very disturbed woman, though her deranged personality was only ever exhibited through anger. Whenever she lost her temper she would scream and shout.

It took no time at all for local children, and a number of young adults who ought to have known better, to turn her into a figure of fun. In order to produce the required reaction they would, on an almost daily basis, bait her. They did it by hurling stones at her door or knocking and running away, and it never failed. Unable to control her responses, Sarah was unable to do anything other than react. That meant she screamed, shouted and hurled abuse whilst the perpetrators hid. It was cruel and humiliating but mental illness in the nineteenth century was not widely recognised and certainly not understood. Add to that

Little Staunton as it looks today. The author

Sarah's manic appearance: only two teeth, unkempt and poor quality clothes, and perhaps it's easier to understand how her neighbours came to consider her condition fair game. What no one could ever have expected was that the level of abuse would escalate and one day end in murder. But old Sally was vulnerable in so many ways.

At a little after nine o'clock on Wednesday 30 November 1870, Sarah's niece, Emma Cariss, made her usual call on her aunt as she had done on numerous mornings in the past. Over the years it had become somewhat of a routine to check on her well being each day. Living as she did, Sarah had few visitors, mainly because most were refused access, Emma being one of the few exceptions. Therefore, it had fallen to her to keep a watchful eye over the old woman's general health, which she seemed happy enough to do. The morning calls were really Sarah's link with the outside world. Emma would fill her in on the local gossip, check she had enough food to eat and, if necessary, get a fire going in the kitchen, though before she could get into the house she would have to follow a proven routine. All too well aware of Sarah's reaction to callers, it had become the norm each day for Emma to tap on the kitchen window before knocking at the door, then announce herself by shouting out her name. That way Sarah knew not to respond angrily when Emma let herself in. But on this particular morning when Emma arrived at the house it was to find all the usual precautions rendered unnecessary. For some strange reason it appeared Sarah had left the front door wide open, something Emma knew was totally out of character. Nervously, she called out and, when she received no response, cautiously entered the house. Sarah Marshall's body lay dead across the bed, her feet hanging over the end, her head on the floor, her torso at an angle on top of the bedclothes and beneath where she lay blood had pooled, staining the floorboards red. It was clear she had died a violently.

Determining just how she had been attacked should have been a relatively straightforward exercise had her body been left alone. Unfortunately, local constable Thomas Sturges had never attended a murder scene. When he arrived at the house some thirty minutes later, concerned for Sally's modesty, he had her body moved and placed in the centre of the bed. That meant when surgeon Joseph Hemming arrived, the nearest to a forensic pathologist the police had, he was placed at a disadvantage. All he could do was list the various injuries. What he could not do was in any way recreate the murder. With nothing more to be gained by leaving Sarah where she lay he had her moved and later that day carried out a full post-mortem.

In his report to police the following day he was at least able to confirm that she had sustained significant injuries. The state of the body also indicated that she had died some twelve hours prior to his arrival, which placed her murder at around midnight on 29 November. According to his autopsy report, Sarah had first been attacked from behind, the lower part of her back being covered in small bruises and lacerations. Horrifically, she had then sustained considerable injuries internally to her bowels after her anus had been penetrated by a blunt instrument. But, he stated, this had not caused her death. Sarah Marshall had died as a result of strangulation.

Little Staunton was then much as it is today, a small village where almost everyone knew everyone else. Police seemed to take the view from the outset of their investigation that the murderer had been local – a reasonable assumption based on the geographical location of the village and its relative isolation in regard to others across the county. They felt that it was highly likely Sarah knew her killer, though there was absolutely no evidence to support that notion. More than likely, it was just a stab in the dark. Certainly, closer inspection of the ground around her cottage had revealed footprints and a clear trail from the rear up a slight bank and through a hedgerow, all the prints having been made by a man wearing hob nailed boots. This alone was probably responsible for deciding initially to keep enquiries local, as the footprints were a clear indicator that whoever had left them seemed to know that from the hedge it was possible to return into the village. Anyone from the outside, so the logic ran, would have gone a different route. But of course at that juncture they had no idea whether the footprints had been made before or after Sarah's murder. Police were simply being pragmatic and it was a reasonable stance to have taken, particularly after a further examination of the ground discovered an imprint of corduroy. Constable Sturges, the man responsible for moving the body, then redeemed himself.

He postulated the theory that the man who had scrambled up the banking was not only the killer but had done so for only one reason: that he lived in one of the cottages that could be seen from the gap in the hedge. Not necessarily the most plausible of theories, but when it came to the village and its inhabitants, Sturges was a very erudite man. He knew his beat, and those that populated it, very well. To believe the killer would never have left so obvious a clue behind, in his opinion, gave the killer

Little Staunton viewed from the church gate. The author

a level of sophistication he knew he did not possess. So, as far as he was concerned the nearest cottage to that gap was the home of Sarah's murderer. Following the logic took him to the door of twenty-year-old William Bull.

Bull was a farm labourer and a man of unsavoury reputation, disliked by many in the village, though exactly why remains a mystery; and was obviously known to Sturges. So when the policeman interviewed him on 30 November it is hard to believe that he had not been influenced by Bull's past, even though Sturges appears never to have doubted his guilt. Bull, who must have expected the visit, obviously denied any involvement. He told the constable that he had been drinking at the local pub and had arrived back home at around 10 pm, a story his mother corroborated. But not a story supported by his fellow drinkers.

They confirmed that in actual fact he had not left the pub until around a quarter-past ten that night. One of them, James Maddison, also told Sturges that he had stood in the street talking to him until after 10.30 pm. At that point, Maddison told the policeman, Bull had told him:

I think I shall go and call old Sally up.

That was damning enough to cause Sturges to make an arrest, which he attempted to do on the following day – but Bull had disappeared. It was a further forty hours before police had him in a cell. At that point they also took away all his clothing for examination. By this time, Dr Hemming had also told them the amount of blood present on the bedroom floor indicated bloodstaining on the killer's clothes. One week later, the theory was substantiated after chemical tests found blood on Bull's jacket and trousers.

The trial opened in Bedford on 15 March 1871 before Mr Justice Blackburn and a packed courtroom. Throughout his incarceration Bull had pleaded his innocence and maintained that plea from his place in the dock, not unexpected by those that had succeeded in finding a seat in the public gallery. Local newspapers kept the public updated on Bull's situation and they would have been surprised had he suddenly admitted guilt. In fact, as the day progressed, it seemed to some that there was little evidence in support of the prosecution. A number of witnesses told of the circumstances surrounding the discovery of Sarah's body. Two neighbours told of how they had heard screams at midnight but disregarded them because

The entrance to Bedford Prison. The author

they came from old Sally's cottage. Dr Hemming reiterated the facts of his post-mortem examination and Bull's fellow drinkers described the night in the local pub and the time he had left to go home. But no witness placed Bull anywhere near the scene of the crime. In fact the only contentious issue for the defence was the fact that blood had been found on his clothing. Unfortunately for justice, science in 1871 was unable to differentiate between blood of an animal and that of a human, which meant that whilst such a finding seemed to substantiate the prosecution contention that it was blood from Sarah, there was no way of proving it. Bull's defence barrister had argued that the blood had come from rats killed at a nearby farm on the same day of the murder and supportive witnesses were produced. The prosecution on the other hand had countered that argument by showing that none of his fellow drinkers had noticed blood on his clothing in the pub. If the staining had taken place during the day ought not these men to have noticed?

In the defence's closing speech at the close of the trial it was these same bloodstains that caused the greatest anxiety:

. . . I ask you gentlemen, if there is a suspicion, if there is a grave suspicion in your minds as to the prisoners guilt, whatever your suspicions may be, whatever your doubts may be, if you are not fully satisfied in your minds that the case has been proved – proved up to the hilt – beyond any possible doubt, do not shrink from your duty, but say that the prisoner at the bar is not guilty, and has not been proved guilty of the crime of which he has been charged . . .

It was a concern shared by the judge also but not one shared by the jury. After an adjournment of twenty minutes they returned a guilty verdict.

They were proved justified in their verdict two weeks later. On 27 March, Bull finally admitted his guilt when he told prison governor Robert E Roberts that he had murdered Sarah Marshall:

. . . She undone the door and stood in the doorway swearing at me and called me a bloody hen roost robber. I then went to the stile near the door, when she struck at me with a long sweeping broom, and struck me on the shoulder, when the broom head fell off . . . I followed her when she hit me a second time with the broom handle . . . When she hit me second time I hit her with my right hand on the head and she fell to the ground. I immediately got on top of her. She was swearing at me . . . I got hold of her throat with my left hand to prevent her shouting and screaming . . . She kicked about, but could not holla as I had tight hold of her throat, and that killed her . . .

Six days later, at eight o'clock on the morning of 3 April 1871, William Bull was led to the scaffold and executed in the prison grounds.

CHAPTER 6

The Body in the Bag

The Case of Lucy Lowe
Stagsden, 1876

. . . she suffocated the baby.

Lucy Lowe, as she eventually became known, was born Lucy Riddy on 28 March 1841 to a poor family in Stagsden. She was the sixth child of a family that by 1853 had swollen to twelve, though four of them never made it beyond the age of nine. Life was certainly tough. Father, Henry, had spent all his life working as an agricultural labourer, which meant he was reliant on local farms for work, though jobs were generally plentiful. Being a labour intensive industry throughout much of the nineteenth century, ensured there was always an income. It was the level of income that often proved inadequate and was eventually supplemented by the girls in the family who all went into lacemaking as they reached teenage years, an occupation some of them maintained throughout their life. Not so, Lucy.

In December 1860, twenty years old and pregnant, she married Samuel Ellis, a local man known by the family who, like her father, worked on nearby farms. Initially the two of them went off to live in Kempston but returned after only a month through lack of work and his declining health, both being forced to move back in with Lucy's parents. Not a perfect solution but not unusual for the period. Unfortunately, three months later, Samuel, who had been a sickly man throughout their short marriage, died. For Lucy it was a devastating blow and most probably changed her view of life forever. Her son, Henry Samuel, was born a month later. For the next four years she continued to work as a lacemaker, help run the home and take care of her son. Then she met the man who would change her life forever.

Ellis Lowe (or Low) had lived all his life in the village of Wootton, some two or three miles south of Stagsden. Probably

Stagsden village today. The author

the two families knew each other. His own family life had almost mirrored that of Lucy. His father, Thomas, was a farm labourer as was he and both his elder brothers. So it was likely that at some point they had all met or at least been aware of each other's existence. That meant there was a sort of commonality between them, which in turn perhaps made their relationship more meaningful. Certainly, Lucy had no hesitation in accepting his proposal of marriage and the two exchanged vows on 20 July 1865.

At that point Lucy left Stagsden, but not with her son Henry; he was left behind in the care of her parents. No place for him in her new family home. She did as was expected and moved to Wootton. Over the next five years they had two children, both girls, though one died in infancy, and there they stayed until 1870. At some point during that year Ellis took a job in Kempston and the family moved. But cracks were beginning to appear in their relationship and arguments more frequent than they had been. Still they stayed together and in 1871 Lucy gave birth to a third child, Ada, and that was followed by a fourth in

Wooton village viewed from St Mary's church. The author

spring, 1873. But for husband Ellis it was all too much. Just what went wrong in the Lowe household is not now known but in June, only weeks after Lucy had given birth, he packed his bags and left. Alone, with no income and a family in need of support, one can only image how desperate Lucy's situation had become. Her solution was, nevertheless, radical. She placed all three surviving children in the workhouse and left for the north of England where she went into domestic service and there she stayed for two years.

In September 1875, desperate to be nearer home, though not necessarily because of her children, she answered a job advert for a cook. The position, which was in Hampstead, meant the occasional trip back to Bedford would be easier, quicker and cheaper than from the north. With a reasonably good employment record behind her and no mention of either her failed marriage or her children, she had little difficulty securing the job. No doubt anonymity gave her a distinct advantage. Had the post been in or around Bedford chances were someone at some point would have cast a dark shadow across her past. As it was she began work for the Reverend Joshua Kirkham and his wife a month later. But what the Kirkhams did not know was that Lucy was five months pregnant when she moved in. Their relationship with their new cook was to be short-lived.

During the Christmas holiday, some eight weeks after her arrival, she told Mrs Kirkham that she had received bad news from her family back in Bedford. So bad in fact that it necessitated her leaving the vicarage in the new year to travel to Bedfordshire and move into her uncle's dairy farm. With the farm to run, she lied, and children to care for, he could not cope and the family were desperate for her to return. The Kirkham's were devastated and, despite what they saw as a family need, did their utmost to dissuade her. But Lucy played her role as family saviour well, insisting she must sacrifice her own future to safeguard her uncle's farm. That won over the vicar and his wife. Deeply impressed by Lucy's apparent sense of duty and obligation they reluctantly accepted her notice and on the 3 January 1876 she left.

But of course she was not heading off to any farm nor was she about to descend on her parents. Instead, she took lodgings with a Mrs Priscilla Hull just off Grey Friars, Bedford, and there she stayed for about ten weeks until the baby, a girl, was

Greyfriars, Bedford, as it looks today. The author

born on 27 February. Lucy had told the landlady shortly after her arrival, that after the birth the baby would be 'going north to Derby' as soon as it was able to travel. There, she had told Mrs Hull, the baby would be adopted by her sister. She would then return to Hampstead. As proof that her employers had been fully conversant with her state of health when she had left in January, Lucy then produced several boxes containing baby clothes. All, she insisted, loaned to her by Mrs Kirkham. The clothes had all been stolen but the story had the required impact on Mrs Hull. Magnanimity, she believed, was a great rarity amongst employers when it came to their domestic staff. If one gave clothes of quality to their cook, as the Kirkham's appeared to have done, then her position in the household must be secure. Leastways that was how she saw it and Lucy had done nothing throughout her stay to dispel that notion.

On 14 March Lucy told her landlady that, with the little baby doing well, she had decided to move out and go to stay at her parents house in Stagsden. The reason she gave was that the sister in Derby had written to say she was travelling down on the following day and would take the baby back with her on her return. In light of what Mrs Hull already knew it seemed an eminently sensible thing to do. Far rather the baby be collected than the mother have to make the long journey north. So, she readily agreed to help with the packing and later that same day even took the two of them to Bedford railway station. There, Lucy bought two tickets to Stagsden and Mrs Hull stood on the platform and waved them on their way.

But of course Lucy had no intention of arriving at her parent's house carrying another child when she already had three others still in the workhouse school. On the outskirts of Stagsden, at a place called Stagsden Side-gate, she suffocated the baby. Then, after placing the body inside a paper bag, she wrapped the bag inside a black skirt and hid it amongst shrubbery. From there she walked on to her parent's house and surprised her father. She stayed there for a week and never mentioned the baby or her job in Hampstead.

On 22 March she made a brief return to Mrs Hull's lodging house in Bedford. As far as the landlady was concerned the visit was merely to reassure her about the baby's departure to Derby. In reality, the visit was to collect a packet of cornflour, which she had bought to use in her baby's feed. Ever conscious that if questions were ever raised, she wanted nothing left behind that could in any way incriminate her. Arriving late, she spent the night at Mrs Hull's rather than travel and left on the

Stagsden Side-Gate, the body was discovered in the woodland on the left. The author

following morning. From Bedford she travelled back to Hampstead and later that same day arrived at the Kirkham's door once again. With a story about her uncle having taken in someone else to do his house work, Lucy wormed her way back into her old role and settled down into what she hoped would be a long, and perhaps prosperous future. But what she did not know at that stage was that the body of her baby daughter had already been found, and the search for the mother was well underway.

On 20 March, whilst Lucy was still at her parent's house, gamekeeper William Robinson, had discovered the tragic bundle whilst patrolling the nearby woodland in search of poachers. As she travelled south on the train local surgeon, Dr Swinson, was carrying out the post-mortem, the results of which he gave to the inquest held at the *Railway Swan*, Turvey. They proved conclusively that the baby had been murdered, though, for Lucy, her identity as the mother would probably have forever remained a mystery had it not been for one factor. Shortly after the birth, Mrs Hull had called in local midwife,

Elizabeth Richardson. That situation was her downfall. Within hours of the baby's discovery police had begun a systematic sweep of all nursing and midwifery professions around Bedford. By the end of March they had found Mrs Hull and on 4 April, Police Constable Mardlin arrived outside the vicarage in Hampstead. Lucy was returned to Bedford that same night and charged with murder.

The trial opened in Bedford on 3 July 1876. Lucy, who by this time had been incarcerated for over three months, pleaded not guilty. Her defence was simple enough. She never denied having given birth to the baby found in the parcel, which would have been a difficult stance to have taken even though equally difficult to prove conclusively. No DNA, no effective forensic science and little to be concluded from blood sampling. But no doubt Lucy was wise enough to realise that police having found Priscilla Hull, and then disproved her original version of the baby being adopted, meant denying being the birth mother would have achieved nothing. In fact it would more than likely have sealed her guilt before the trial began. So, she took the defence of accidental death. Lucy claimed that whilst taking the baby to her parent's house it had suffered a seizure. A seizure so bad that she had been unable to save its life. At that point,

Turvey village where the inquest was held. The author

she had told her defence counsel, she had done what many in her situation would have done – she panicked. Afraid of the repercussions, she decided to hide the body. The fact that no one in her family had known of her pregnancy, she insisted, was merely coincidental. But because that had been the case she argued that it would have been impossible to then turn up unannounced at her parent's home and tell them the grandchild that they never knew had existed had already died.

In the circumstances it was a good defence to offer. Science was nowhere near the level it has reached today, therefore it was extremely difficult to disprove anything she said. They had found the body, they had discovered it had died from suffocation. But they had no real conclusive proof that Lucy had been instrumental in its death. No doubt, when the trial began, she believed that there was a real possibility of acquittal. But despite the lack of evidence in support of the police assertion that she had committed murder the jury found her guilty. No doubt mainly because of motive. It was perfectly clear that she had done everything in her power to hide the baby's birth, in fact, hide its very existence. Why, ran the prosecution argument,

St Mary's church, Wooton, where Ellis Lowe was buried in 1894. The author

would a woman do that if she intended the child to live? Was it not because its death had been planned long before Lucy's arrival at the lodging house in Bedford? They were right of course and Lucy Low was sentenced to death.

But from the minute of her conviction a series of appeals were made to have the sentenced commuted to one of life imprisonment. On 19 July, five days before she was due to hang, the reprieve was finally granted.

As a footnote to the case, her husband, the man that had abandoned her and his family years earlier, was admitted to Bedford workhouse in March of 1893 and died less than a year later, aged fifty-nine. He was buried at Wootton. Lucy is recorded by Knaphill Female Convict Prison as having either died or been discharged around 1885. The record is vague but there is a suspicion that she did survive her prison sentence and went to join her daughter somewhere in the north-west of the country.

CHAPTER 7

The Rage of a Silent Man

The Killing of Effie Burgin
Bedford, 1895

Effie was dead almost before her body hit the ground . . .

Born in Eynesbury near St Neots, Effie Burgin made the move to Bedford in 1893. At that time she was eighteen years old and keen to earn her own way through life. Her parents, who stayed behind in Cambridgeshire, were apprehensive but supported the move. This was partly because they recognised their daughter's aspirations and partly because they knew that she would still have access to family support. Her father's sister had married a Bedford man, George Covington, thirty years earlier. Their

Bedford Town c1905. Author's collection

home on Wellington Street was near to where she would be working and their eldest son Arthur was the love of Effie's life. For Effie it was a perfect move.

With her employer, Dr Lloyd, only a five-minute walk away on Harpur Street, she was able to see the Covingtons on a regular basis. In fact, within a few short months she had established a routine that suited everyone. Wellington Street was a regular haunt every Sunday evening after church, and once a fortnight, on a Thursday. That way the couple were always able to get time alone when Arthur walked her home. Not ideal perhaps, but Effie seemed happy enough with it and slowly the relationship blossomed until the besotted Arthur finally asked her to marry him in the summer of 1894. A delighted Effie accepted and the pair announced their engagement in early autumn. But Arthur was not all he seemed.

For most of his life he had suffered with his nerves. On two occasions during the 1880s his father had paid for him to see doctors at Bedford, but they had proved ineffective in their diagnosis and Arthur's flawed character had remained with him into adulthood. Unable to hold down a job because of its effects, despite his father's best efforts, he had drifted in and

Harpur Street, Bedford today. The author

out of work until just after his twentieth birthday. By that time, having been apprenticed to three different High Street clothiers since leaving school, none of whom had managed to hold on to him, he gave up, deciding that work was not something he felt mentally equipped to continue with and became unemployable. When the couple became engaged he had not worked for six years. Instead, his days had been spent at home or in the nearby billiard rooms. Had his father not been head ostler and groom at the *George Hotel*, money would have been in short supply, and his refusal to work a severe handicap to the family. As it was things were often tight financially, but never to the extent that Arthur would be forced out of the family home. Effie either ignored the obvious or chose not to see it. Either way, almost a year after the engagement, her refusal to view Arthur's behaviour with the caution it demanded cost her dearly.

On Thursday evening, 13 June 1895, as had become her normal practice, Effie called to the Covington house on her night off. She, her aunt and uncle, and Arthur had sat around the kitchen table talking until 10 pm, something they had done for the past eighteen months. The clock striking out the hour being her cue to set off back to Harpur Street and, the resumption of her life as a domestic. As the doctor's household rose at six each morning, late nights were not something she could easily afford. After saying her goodbyes she walked out of the kitchen into the living room, which was situated in the centre of the house. Arthur dutifully followed on behind, but this time, as she reached the middle of the room and stooped to pick up her coat from the table, he was not there to help her. Instead, from a distance of no more than six inches he shot her three times in the head. Effie was dead almost before her body hit the ground and she would never have known who had fired the shots. Arthur then knelt down beside her and kissed her three times.

George Covington burst into the room in time to see this bizarre final act of love. There was nothing he could do to save Effie. The gunshot wounds had destroyed much of her head, there was also nothing he could do for his son. Arthur had no explanation for what he had done. In fact he refused to even discuss it. Instead, he simply stood mute, despite his father's pleading, and waited for the arrival of the police who he knew would have been sent for. Alerted by neighbours, local constables Setchell and Chapman, made the arrest within minutes, and a subdued Arthur was taken to Bedford prison.

There, he offered up no explanation for his actions and

Wellington Street, Bedford, where the Covington family lived. The author

refused to make any sort of statement other than an acknowledgement of guilt and demanded an immediate trial. At a loss
as to how and why he should have shot Effie Burgin without
warning, police began the usual round of questioning. But
nothing from any quarter offered up any explanation of
Arthur's actions. The couple had been on good terms. There
were no other suitors, Effie had not spoken to her friends of
problems or difficulties in the relationship, and no one knew
just how Arthur had come to own a gun. To the family's certain
knowledge guns of any kind had never been handled by him nor
had he ever displayed any inclination toward owning one.
Nothing, it appeared, could offer up a motive or account for
Arthur's totally irrational actions.

On the following morning Arthur appeared in Bedford
magistrates' court. Throughout the morning crowds had been
gathering outside Shire Hall, eager to see the face of the man
who had put three bullets into his fiancée. When he finally took
his place in the dock the *Bedfordshire Times And Independent*
described him as, 'looking pale, distressed and trembling very
strongly', hardly surprising given all the circumstances. The
main reason for his appearance was not to try him for murder
but to decide whether or not he would stand trial at the forth-

coming Assizes. They being only three days away, the magistrates needed to be certain that there was a defence team in place and that the prosecution had the time to gather the relevant evidence. Arthur made a misguided attempt to help the decision by refusing to be represented. This, he thought, would directly aid justice. He told the court that he neither wanted nor needed a defence team. Furthermore, he added that he was prepared to go to the assize court and stand trial. But the court, as they had to do, objected to his stance and therefore agreed to remand him into custody for the next four months. That, argued the Bench, would give adequate time for all the evidence to be taken and a defence barrister, despite Arthur's objections, to be placed in charge of the defence. The hearing ended after about one hour, at which point George Covington tried desperately to talk to his son and convince him that he had to take part in his own defence. The effort was doomed to failure; Arthur refused to listen and was eventually taken back to the cells, still insisting there was nothing to defend. But the law was not about to allow him to prejudice his own case.

Bedford's Corn Exchange where the coroner's court was held. The author

As the court hearing ended, the inquest into Effie Burgin's killing began. A number of those who crowded into the court-house transferred to the hall of Bedford's Corn Exchange, which was where the coroner, Dr Prior, had set up his court-room. It was a fairly straightforward affair. Those who saw anything were called to give their account and Mr C G Johnson, surgeon, who had charge of the body, gave a preliminary report. He told the court that there were three distinct bullet wounds and their placement tended to support his view that there would have been no warning of Covington's intent before the gun was fired. Other than that, he told the hearing, he needed more time. The coroner, therefore, aware of the earlier court decision to defer any murder trial until November, decided to adjourn for four days. Not that it made a deal of difference. The final post-mortem results, which the doctor gave when the court sat for the resumption, added nothing further to the case except to say that the third and final shot had been fired after Effie's body had hit the floor. But any of the three shots would have killed her.

On 18 June Effie Burgin was laid to rest in the cemetery attached to her native place, Eynesbury. It was a sad and moving affair. Throughout the early afternoon all roads leading to the church had been choked with mourners, most dressed in black, many having travelled a long way, and all heading toward the three o'clock funeral. Forming the cortège itself, which stretched back into the village, were friends, relatives, and Effie's five sisters and two brothers. The family's request that it be a private affair was lost on the majority. In truth, the depth of anger felt by many at what Arthur Covington had done was never going to allow that to happen. Too many people wanted to show their support to the grieving relatives and at the same time demonstrate their disdain for her killer. For many, justice was going to be a long time coming. When it did come it came with a November fog and heavy rain.

Covington took his place in the dock at a little after ten o'clock in the morning on 14 November 1895. Four months languishing in Bedford Prison had significantly changed his appearance from that seen at the magistrates' hearing in June. When he pleaded not guilty in front of Mr Justice Day he was hardly recognizable as the same man. He had gained weight, lost the trembling nerves and appeared far more alert to his immediate surroundings. A prison regime of exercise and regular meals had clearly improved both his physical and mental well-being. Unfortunately for his defence team, which he had been

Bedford Prison. The author

persuaded to accept, it was perhaps too much of an improvement. Particularly in a man claimed by this same defence counsel to have been insane at the time he fired three bullets into Effie Burgin, a claim the prosecution were almost honour bound to contest. They insisted from the outset that there could be no acceptable argument that Arthur Covington was anything other than sane when he bought the gun, loaded it, aimed it at Effie's head, and fired three times with the intent to kill. Had it been otherwise, they told the court, perhaps he would have aimed to wound, perhaps shot her in the arm or the leg. As it was, they told the jury, he had deliberately aimed at the one place on the human body almost certain to result in death, the head. That meant he was rational, in possession of his faculties and well able to make a decision. A man that is insane, they told the jury, does not possess that ability. Furthermore, they argued, his decision to commit murder must have been made some days prior to the killing. Effie only visited the house twice a week, Sunday and Thursday, which meant Covington had planned the shooting. Insane men cannot do that.

It was a powerful argument and as the day progressed they

succeeded in proving their point, first, by hearing the testimony of Covington's father, George. He had told police and earlier hearings that the shooting had taken place as Effie went to fetch her coat from the living room. What the prosecution brought out was the speed at which the killing took place. Under oath, Covington's father told the court that the shots were immediate. No more than thirty seconds elapsed between Effie saying goodbye and his son firing the fatal shots. That, pointed out the prosecution, meant premeditation.

This was followed by damning testimony from Dr Edward Swain, resident medical superintendent of Arlesey Asylum. He told the court that the results of his medical examination had revealed that Covington knew the difference between right and wrong, which meant he knew it was wrong to take away a life. This was then supported by evidence given by Bedford Prison's own doctor, Mr R Kinsey. He agreed with Swain's testimony and added that throughout his incarceration Covington had exhibited no signs of excitement or depression, had gained one stone in weight, slept well each night, and never demonstrated any tendency toward insanity.

Between the two they had totally wrecked the defence case. For Arthur Covington there were to be no mitigating circumstances acceptable to the court, though the defence, ably led by Mr Hugo Young, made a valiant effort. In his closing speech at the end of the day he told the jurors exactly what the law demanded before a plea of insanity could be accepted:

> *In order to establish a defence on the ground of insanity it must be clearly proved that at the time of committing the act the party accused was labouring under such a defect of reason, from a disease of the mind, that he did not know the value and quality of the act he was doing, or if he did know, did not know he was doing wrong . . .*

That meant, he told them, that it was possible to be insane at the time but not insane at a later date. Arthur Covington, he argued, fitted that bill. Accepting the doctor's evidence as credible, he told the court that any examination made long after the killing was highly likely to have come to the conclusion they had. But had the examination been made hours after the fatal shots had been fired would they not have found a different man? A man clearly delusional, a man with no rational thought in his head, a man who could not then differentiate between right and wrong, and a man who was clearly insane.

It was an understandable argument and perhaps would have gained some merit amongst the jurors had it not been for Mr Justice Day. He was having none of it and told the court it was simply not acceptable to claim a man could be mad one minute and sane the next:

> . . . *Insanity did consist of a man showing a sudden flash of wildness. A man must be insane by reason of disease to such an extent that he did not know the nature or quality of the act that he committed . . . The law presumed that everybody who was charged with any offence was sane, and that until a person, whose mind was said to be diseased or his friends proved that it was so, he was responsible for his actions . . . They [the jury] were not in the box to administer mercy . . .*

When they finally retired it took just twenty minutes to agree and return a guilty verdict. From that moment on George Covington worked tirelessly to obtain a reprieve for his son. He argued vociferously that his son was mentally deranged when he took the revolver and fired at the woman he loved. That, he insisted, had been borne out by his physical state when he appeared before Bedford magistrates immediately after his arrest. If the examination into his mental condition had been made at that point there would never have been a trial. It may well have been a valid point but there was little support for his point of view amongst most in the county. To local people, Arthur Covington was a murderer, a man who had killed a young woman and who had never demonstrated the kind of mental collapse his father believed he had suffered.

Covington was executed at eight o'clock on the morning of 3 December 1895, within the walls of Bedford Prison, by hangman James Billington. The deceased left behind no written statement or ever confessed his guilt.

CHAPTER 8

Too Drunk to Know

The Murder of Harriet Reeve
Leighton Buzzard, 1915

The scene inside the kitchen was truly horrific.

It is probably fair to say that William Reeve had done little by way of work for most of his life, preferring instead to stay home or in the nearest pub when money allowed, which was more often than it ought to have been. That money generally came from his wife, Harriett. Of the two it was her who had the only permanent job, working three hours a day for 9d [4p]. William would claim that

The White Hart, *Hockliffe*. The author

The Stag, *Leighton Buzzard.* The author

he supplemented her pay by working as a paid drover for local farms around Leighton Buzzard, taking livestock to market every Tuesday. Poorly paid and income far from regular, Harriet would probably never have agreed, all too well aware that this one day's work usually represented five days' drinking. She knew well enough that the only person likely to see the colour of William's money was the landlord of the local pub. So, with six children to clothe and feed, life in the Reeve household was never going to be easy.

By the autumn of 1915, as the French army celebrated victory at the battle of the Marne and saved Paris from falling into German hands, the Reeve's marriage was at breaking point. William, by now a somewhat bitter forty-two-year-old, wanted life to end. He had had enough of the daily grind, the constant lack of money and the never ending arguments. For him the relationship was at an end and had been for years. But unlike today, divorce in 1915 was for those that had the money to pay. William had none. So they stayed together. It is also fair to say that from a purely personal point of view he knew he would be disadvantaged by any legal closure on his marriage. If Harriett were not there, that three shillings and nine pence she earned every week would not be there for him to tap when he needed cash. But things were about to get much worse.

At around half-past eight on the morning of 5 July 1915 William, having already downed two pints of beer, met neighbour Thomas Major in the street trying to hold onto a dog. Major explained to him that he had found it roaming the streets during the night, but added that it was no ordinary pet. It belonged to the landlord of the *White Hart* at Hockliffe, and that made it special. If they returned it, there would be a reward and that reward would be in beer. William needed no persuading and an hour later the two men were drinking the first of two free pints. From Hockliffe they walked to nearby Eggington and the *Plough Inn,* then on to the *Falcon* followed by the *Roebuck* at Leighton Buzzard. By that time it was three o'clock in the afternoon and the two men had supped some eight pints of beer each. For Major that was enough and he called time and staggered off home. But for William, a hardened drinker, the day had only just begun. He made for the *Stag Inn* where he settled into a game of dominoes that lasted until just after 6 pm. Then, too drunk to continue and wary of going home, he made his way to his nephew's house. There, in a drunken stupor, he told nephew Jack Toms that he had no money and Harriett had refused to give him any so he was going to kill her. But Toms had grown up with William's frequent bouts of drunkenness. He knew all too well that alcohol always made him garrulous but never dangerous, so he ignored the threat. Sitting William by the fire to calm him down, he sent one of his own children off to his aunt's house on Plantation Road to see if Harriett had arrived home from work. When the boy returned to say she had, he packed William off home, probably relieved to see the back of him. What he could never have imagined was that William had made no idle threat.

At around half-past six that night, he walked into the kitchen of the family home. There was no argument, no confrontation, no quarrel. In fact, Harriet never even spoke to her husband. At the time, all the children were out except their eldest son and, perhaps expecting trouble, Harriet gave him sixpence and sent him off to the cinema. Then she calmly sat in her usual chair by the table. William, ostracized by his wife, sat in the only other chair on the other side of the room and lit a cigarette. Five minutes later, with still not a flicker of acknowledgement from Harriet, he calmly reached behind his chair, retrieved his shotgun, which had been loaded earlier in the day, stood up and fired both barrels at her head. She was killed instantly. Suddenly shocked by the realization of what he had done and before neighbours could react, he then took a cut-throat razor from its place on the mantelpiece and slit his own throat. There it ought to have ended. But William, whilst good with a gun was more than useless with a razor. Unable to inflict a wound deep enough to cause haemorrhage, he then stumbled around the house unable to harm himself a second time, and eventually staggered out into the street straight into the arms of Police Constable William Clark.

Clark part carried, part dragged William to a house across the street. There he rendered first aid, called for a doctor, and when satisfied the injuries were not life threatening, made his way back to the Reeve house. The scene inside the kitchen was truly horrific. Harriett still sat at the table by the window, her left leg crossed over her right, her elbow resting on the table top as if she were looking out across the yard. But the bottom part of her right cheek had been blown away, exposing the jaw, and there was a large, round hole at the base of her neck. Much of the plaster on the wall behind her had been shot away, and the curtains were completely saturated with her blood. Outside, he

Plantation Road, Leighton Buzzard as it looks today. The author

found the shotgun that had killed her, ammunition that matched it and the blood-soaked cut-throat razor.

It was a reasonably straightforward case for Bedfordshire police. A number of close neighbours were able to testify as to the time of the murder. The general consensus of opinion being that William had fired the gun at about a quarter to seven that night. Too many were able to attest to his inebriated state, having seen him stagger home, and the various pub landlords that had served him throughout the day were able to quantify the amount of alcohol he had consumed. All in all there was very little going for William when he stood in the dock three months later.

However, it did not stop him entering a not guilty plea when he stood in front of Mr Justice Shearman on 19 October. Throughout his incarceration he had considered his defence well. Faced with the prospect of execution and suffering from partial amnesia brought on by the beer, he went for the only real option to murder – accidental death. In lengthy discussions with his defence counsel, Mr William Burkett, he told him that he had no real memory of events surrounding his wife's death. He accepted his drunken state at the time of the shooting, but claimed not to have harboured any thoughts of murder. Contrary to all the testimony eventually heard in court, he argued that his marriage was strong. At no time, he insisted, had he ever contemplated leaving the family home or breaking his wedding vows. This was complete and utter rubbish, with little chance of being corroborated by the prosecution witnesses brought to court by the Crown. But, nevertheless, a defence he insisted to be the truth.

By the afternoon session, as expected, his version of married bliss and accidental shooting had been completely discredited. With little else to throw into the court arena the defence counsel decided to put William on the stand. In front of a packed court-room he told the judge that he had never intended harm to his wife. The dialogue was as follows:

Mr Burkett: *Can you remember anything that happened in that room on the night of Monday, July 5?*

Reeve: *No, I cannot remember anything that happened there.*

Mr Burkett: *Had you any intention of injuring your wife in any way?*

Reeve: *No sir, I hadn't. God forbid. She was the best friend I had got.*

Mr Burkett:	*Can you tell these gentlemen* [the jurors] *why you cut your throat in the way that had been described, so that your life was despaired of?*
Reeve:	*The only thing was that when I was going out with the gun it must have gone off, and I caught up the razor, and I was horrified, and I cut my throat.*
Mr Burkett:	*However vague your recollection is about that night – are you quite clear that you had no intention of doing your wife any harm at all?*
Reeve:	*I am certain I hadn't, sir.*

He went on to explain to the court that the gun itself was faulty and when the right barrel was fired the left went off automatically, which was why Harriet had received such horrific wounds, not because that was what he had intended. He also denied that he had ever told his nephew that he intended to kill

The Shire Hall, Bedford where Reeve stood trial. The author

his wife, though he had to admit that his mind was not totally clear as to just what he had said. None of it made a great deal of difference.

When defence counsel stood in front of the jury at the close of the day to make the obligatory impassioned speech for clemency, he must have known his case was lost. But he did point out to the jury one very salient fact. No one had actually seen the shooting. They may have heard it from a distance, may have expected William to at some point attack his wife, but no one was in the room when the shooting took place. That, according to William Burkett, was a key fact and one the jury must not lose sight of. In an eloquent speech, he told them there were only two possible outcomes for their verdict. The first one was murder, but to prove it there had to have been sufficient evidence of motive and intent. Neither, argued the barrister, existed. When the body of Harriet Reeve had been found, he went on, she was still sitting at the table. All indicators pointed toward her having absolutely no knowledge of what was to happen to her. If it had been murder would she not have moved, fought, screamed, attempted to disarm Reeve? But she did not. Therefore, he reasoned, her death had to have been as a result of an accident. That, he urged, was the only possible verdict in light of all the evidence and circumstances surrounding the death.

It was valid up to a point. Certainly no one saw it but simply because there was no fight did not mean there was no murderous intent. The jury recognised that point and after a short adjournment William Reeve was found guilty and sentenced to death.

On Tuesday 16 November over one hundred people braved snow and a keen northerly wind to gather outside Bedford Prison. There was nothing to see. Reeve made the short journey to the scaffold unseen by the outside world and was executed by John Ellis at precisely eight o'clock in the morning. As the clock chimes fell away the crowd huddled against the cold arctic blast and then slowly slipped away to carry on their daily lives, satisfied that for Harriett Reeve justice had been done.

CHAPTER 9

A Soldier's Tale

The Death of Amy Martin
Luton, 1915

Striking out with his right hand, he stabbed her once in the neck.

Henry Charles Martin joined the Royal Artillery regiment in April 1915, not because he wanted to fight for king and country, nor because he had a desire for glory. Private Martin, as he became, took the king's shilling because he wanted to escape his wife. More so, he wanted to escape what his wife had threatened to do. Since the couple had moved with their three children from Barking to Luton, his life had been turned upside down – due in large part because of her desire to aid the war effort and his initial reluctance to go into uniform. Amy Martin wanted to do her bit. So, she had convinced her husband, at the start of the year, to allow her to open up their house to lodgers. Those lodgers would all be temporary and all in the armed services. But when Henry had agreed to her plan he had never considered that one of these young soldiers would break his marriage apart.

After thirteen years married, Amy sought adventure, something new and different in her life. Being a wife and mother was all well and good but she had decided that there was more to life and she intended to grab it. So, dissatisfied, unhappy and probably desperate to bring love and affection back into her life, she embarked upon an affair. Like all affairs it began in secret; a clandestine relationship conducted during the hours of darkness and as far away from prying eyes as it was possible to be. But then, like all affairs, a mistake here, a wrong word there and the secret began to slip. Meetings in lonely places became meetings in her own home, people noticed, neighbours talked and eventually the affair was uncovered.

Initially, it was her children who noticed a different behaviour in their mother. Then she was caught in an embrace with a soldier they knew – but not as their father. Finally, she

Bedford Road, Luton c1910. Author's collection

was caught by her brother making love in the kitchen and the game was up. Within days, Henry had been told and in the inevitable confrontation that followed Amy admitted that she was in love with a soldier from the Lincolnshire regiment. He was named Newbury.

At the time Henry discovered the truth there was little he could do. Based in Stratford and with restricted leave throughout that summer, he was forced to confine his anger to letters. These he sent to the house at Blythe Place, Luton. But most of the letters never reached Amy. At some point in early August 1915 she had moved without telling him in the hope that she could disappear from her marriage. But it was never likely to work. On 1 October, some eight weeks after her house move, Henry arrived back in Luton with a two-day pass. A short walk from the railway station brought him to an empty house and neighbours all too ready to fill in the gaps in his knowledge. The affair, it seemed, was by this time common knowledge, as was Amy's new location. Henry, who of course already knew a great deal about his wife's infidelity, was more angered by her deceit. He wanted a confrontation. She had humiliated him, taken his family, his furniture, even his clothes and cast him aside as if he were excess baggage. Fortunately for her, when he found the new house, which was on nearby Queen Street, it was locked up and, despite several attempts, he failed to break in. So, somewhat despondent, he left and slept rough that night and returned in the morning. By then he was much calmer.

When the two of them finally met there was no fight, no argument, no raised words, just a reasoned discussion. Henry did his best to remain impassive, though it was no doubt difficult, and perhaps for the first time Amy was honest. She told him that she had fallen in love with Newbury and could not give him up, that her brother had caught them together and, since his departure to France, she had been writing to him and sending out cigarettes and handkerchiefs. Furthermore, she told Henry, the two of them planned to emigrate to Australia. It was probably at that point Henry understood for the first time that his marriage was finally over. But not just in a conventional sense. Australia is on the other side of the world. In 1915 jet aircraft were only a distant dream and travel on a global scale was virtually impossible. In turn that meant no future reconciliation, no children, and no family. Henry was devastated.

That night he slept fully clothed on top of the bed beside his wife. He was to catch a London train in the early hours and rejoin his regiment. It was never likely to happen, given his emotional turmoil and state of mind. At half-past four in the morning, aware the train was long gone, he went down to the kitchen. There he made tea for the two of them, cut himself a slice of bread using his army knife, and returned to the bedroom. Amy was awake, like Henry her sleep had been fitful at best, but unlike her husband when she opened her eyes, all that shone from them was bitterness and anger. Grudgingly, she accepted the tea. Then, in a spiteful, vindictive attack, told him to leave. Baiting him from the bed, she pointed an accusing finger at him and threatened that it would be the last time he ever stayed at the house. Then she mentioned Australia. That was enough for Henry. Striking out with his right hand, he stabbed her once in the neck. Bleeding profusely, Amy screamed, scrambled out of bed and ran to her next door neighbours. They did what they could but too much damage had been done.

Whilst all this was going on Henry simply walked out into the street and surrendered himself to the first policeman he found. He never denied his guilt. There was little point, though he did say that the killing had been accidental. According to Henry's statement, when he had returned to the bedroom with the tea he still had his army knife in his hand. Striking out at Amy had,

Blythe Place, Luton today. The author

he insisted, been a reflex action and he had not realised at the time that he still gripped the knife. If he had intended to murder her he would have done a better job. Then, he told police, he would have run away. Until he had seen the blood he claimed not to have realised he had stabbed her at all, which was why he went in search of a policeman.

Constable Henshaw, the policeman he surrendered to, took a pragmatic view. Whether Amy was alive or dead was not his initial concern. He had a possible killer in front of him and that took precedence. So, Henry was marched off to Luton police station where he could be secured and, once there, Henshaw sought help from Police Inspector Peter James. The two men eventually arrived at the house as Amy was being taken off to hospital where she later died. What they found surprised them and tended to support Henry's version of events. The bedroom showed no signs of a struggle, her teacup had been placed on the small table beside the bed, nothing had been broken or thrown and the bed itself was still made and in good order. All of which appeared to reinforce Henry's brief verbal account of what had happened in the house on Queen Street. But ever

sceptical, they then carried out a reasonably thorough examination of the room in search of anything that might contradict
or help interpret the murder scene differently. They found very
little, six shillings and sixpence under the mattress, a small
brooch, a pawn ticket, Henry's army knife, and an Imperial
Service brooch. Though they did not realise it at the time, this
last item was to later prove significant, enquiries eventually
proving it had once belonged to private Newbury.

Henry eventually made a full written statement in which he
detailed the problems he had suffered in his marriage, the arguments over the past months and Amy's confession to an affair.
But in it he also continued to maintain that death had been
accidental. Later that same day partial support came his way
from an unlikely source. Dr Charles Lewis, who had carried out
a post-mortem on Amy's body, told police that the wound itself
was only 1¾ inches deep [4cm]. No great pressure had been
applied in causing it and Amy's death had been as a result of
the knife being withdrawn. If the knife had remained in the
wound then, in his opinion, Amy would have survived. But
when Henry had pulled his hand away the knife blade had
nicked the main external jugular vein. The real injury was done
not so much by the incision as in the withdrawal.

When Henry Martin took his place in the dock on Monday
morning, 18 October, charged with murder, he knew there was
a better than even chance he would never face the gallows. The
discovery of the brooch under the mattress and the name of its
owner, had given credence to his account of Amy's infidelity. It
meant no prosecution counsel could accuse him of believing
vague innuendo or acting on impulse fuelled by stories of an
imagined affair. The evidence in support of his account of
marital disharmony had been found and had been placed in the
public arena, though what he knew he had to clearly prove was
that he had never intended to commit murder. This second
point was the one that was obviously going to be the most difficult to prove. Although with the medical evidence and the
amount of provocation he claimed he had endured, it seemed
that the court were more predisposed to believe rather than
disbelieve, and so it proved. In the defence counsel's closing
speech at the end of the short trial he told the jury that it was
this latter point they had to consider closely:

> . . . *Where provocation has been so recent as in this case, they*
> *might reasonably assume that at the time the wound was given*
> *the prisoner was not master of his own understanding; or that he*

was taunted beyond all endurance and forgot himself, and then your verdict should be one of manslaughter only. I imagine that it was one of the saddest stories you have ever heard. The one thing outstanding in it was not a desire on the husband's part to take her life, but a heartfelt desire for her to give up her affection for Newbury and go back and live in the old happy way . . .

The judge appeared to have the utmost sympathy for the defence's view and in his summing up told the jury they could consider returning a manslaughter verdict if they felt it reasonable to do so:

You must not find the most serious verdict of murder unless you are satisfied that the evidence justifies it, and it would be your privilege and duty if you thought when you had weighed the evidence that the prisoner did not of malice and forethought kill this poor woman . . . It was in his favour that the knife was not bought for the purpose, but was the sort that soldiers and sailors carried with them. The law says it is open to the jury to reduce the charge to that of manslaughter if they thought that the provocation which was given at the moment was such as to lead a man to do something that he never really intended to do, even though he takes up a dangerous weapon . . .

The jury took little persuading and after a few minutes adjournment returned a verdict of *manslaughter under great provocation.* Henry Martin was sentenced to twelve months in prison.

Chapter 10

A Date With Death

The Mysterious Case of Ellen Rault
Haynes Camp, 1919

She was laid on her back, with her legs doubled up under her . . .

At the end of the First World War Britain still had a million men in uniform. Most wanted to return to their families and pick up the pieces of their lives as best they could. To aid this process the army camp at Haynes, a few miles south of Bedford, was used in part as a demobilisation point where soldiers were brought before being demobbed, and returned to civilian life. It was also used as the training ground for new recruits and young cadets intent on making the army their future career. In support of all these

Wilstead Woods. The author

activities were the women who formed Queen Mary's Army Auxiliary Corps. Small in number, theirs was very much a hands-on role, running the laundry, maintaining food supplies, operating the various canteens and the officers' mess. As such they were an integral part of the smooth running of the camp. They were also young, generally single and like most young people keen to mix with the opposite sex. As an aid almost to better relations between the ranks, camp dances were set up at least twice a week. There they could meet, chat, dance and have a few drinks in a less formal atmosphere. Occasionally, relation-ships were formed, though rarely were these serious, and often groups would arrange to meet off site. Bedford was the town of choice, only a short walk away, beyond Wilstead Woods, which formed the camp's northern perimeter.

Twenty-one-year-old Ellen Rault, 'Nelly' to her friends, moved into the camp in the spring of 1918. A member of the

The road from Haynes toward Wilstead Woods today. The author

Corps since summer of the previous year, she had travelled from her family's home on Jersey to the mainland because she wanted to help the war effort. Whether life as a cook in the officers' mess was quite what she had in mind is probably debateable but, nevertheless, she made no attempt to leave, even choosing to stay on after the war had ended because of the friends she had made. There is no doubt Ellen enjoyed her life in the military, especially the camaraderie, though her parents had understandable reservations about the life she had chosen. In her weekly letters home she had tried hard to put their minds at rest, always enthusing about life on the camp, always being upbeat about the events in her week, despite the boring repetitiveness of her days in the makeshift kitchens. Quiet, unassuming, but with a love of the great outdoors, Ellen had found the freedoms she enjoyed a fair compensation for the routines she endured and always took advantage of whatever spare time she could garner, Bedford and its river being a favoured place. These frequent trips generally being made alone, not for reasons of indifference, more to do with the army and its inflexible duty rosters. When Ellen was listed to work her friends often were not and vice versa. So, over the months she had grown accustomed to her own company. The only social time she spent with her various girlfriends tended to be at the camp's evening dances. As for men, other than as passing acquaintances and those she knew by name because she served them food each day, there were none. Leastways, none she had formed any serious relationship with, although Ellen was known to favour the company of one particular officer.

At some point early in 1919 she had danced with Colour Sergeant Major Hepburn. He was a tall, dark, taciturn man, known by his colleagues to usually shun the company of women and almost never attend the weekly dances. So just how or why he attended the one where the two of them met is a bit of a mystery. Perhaps she had invited him along, perhaps he had wanted to meet her and the dance was the only place. Either way, once they had met they began to spend more time in each other's company, though it appears the relationship was nothing other than platonic, or at least that was how Ellen viewed it. She liked the sergeant major, enjoyed his company and occasionally walked into Bedford with him but it was no love match – something Ellen had never hidden and something her friends were well aware of. To them, the association was a source of amusement, not maliciously so, more because the two were so opposite. Hepburn's reputation as a loner being at odds

The Embankment at Bedford as Ellen would have seen it c1915. Author's collection

with Ellen's friendly, affable character. To those who knew her it all seemed so incongruous.

On Thursday 8 May 1919, at the first spring dance of the year, as had become the norm by now, the pair of them danced together all night. At the close of the evening Ellen, who knew she would be free from mid-afternoon on the following day, asked the sergeant major if he would like to spend it with her in Bedford. If the weather was good she wanted to walk by the river and then probably hire a bicycle to ride back before dark, something she had done before. He readily agreed and it was arranged that to save a long walk they would both hitch a lift on the NAAFI lorry. It left camp every Friday afternoon as a matter of routine between half-past three and five o'clock to fetch supplies from Bedford town centre; the 'camp taxi' as it had become known.

At about a quarter to four in the afternoon next day, Hepburn met Ellen just inside the camp gate. She told him the lorry was delayed and she was going to set off on foot. She had with her a poetry book and told Hepburn she would probably stop en route and read a little. They talked for a few minutes then the sergeant major, who had already explained that he still needed a few minutes before he could get away, told her he would still hitch the lift and get the lorry to pick her up on the way. He then returned to his duties in the demobilisation hut whilst Ellen went out of the camp gates and off along the road beside Wilstead Woods. At around a quarter to five the lorry finally left, Hepburn sat on the back and it set out for Bedford. It never passed Ellen. According to the sergeant major's later testimony, when he arrived in town he went straight to the river to see if she had somehow arrived earlier and, after a fruitless search, returned to camp around 9 pm.

For the next two days the army did nothing. Ellen was reported missing on the Saturday morning, not by Hepburn but by the girls who knew she ought to have been back in her bed by lights out on the Friday. But the army took the view, understandably perhaps, that she had just gone absent without leave. It appears she had done that once the previous year. But as Monday dawned with still no sign of the missing girl, a search party of one hundred soldiers was organised and sent into the nearby woodland. At 3.35 pm that afternoon her body was discovered just inside Wilstead Woods some fifteen yards from the Bedford road. She lay on her back, with her legs doubled up under her, as if she had been on her knees and fallen backward. Her right arm was outstretched and by the hand was a clean

Bedford town c1905. Author's collection

dinner knife. Her left hand clutched her left breast and her skirt was above her waist. She had been partially covered over with several small tree branches, which had been broken off a nearby hazel tree. She had been stabbed four times in the chest, one of the wounds piercing her heart, and there were other wounds on her face, arms, neck; and a single stab wound to her back. When Police Constable Holben arrived on the scene he searched Ellen's clothing and found in her tunic a purse containing ten shillings and threepence [52p] and two hand-kerchiefs. According to his later report, the ground for some six feet all around where she lay had also been trampled down and showed clear signs of there having been a struggle.

Dr Langham Garner was brought from Ampthill to examine the body in situ, before carrying out a full post-mortem. The report of his findings showed that there was almost no blood on the ground when the body was lifted, indicative of death being almost instantaneous. Furthermore, contrary to popular belief at the time, Ellen had not been raped or suffered any kind of sexual molestation. In the later autopsy he found that all the chest wounds were above the top of her corset and had been made with a downward thrust, suggestive of a killer who was taller than Ellen. The perpetrator was also someone who had intended to murder not just wound, the knife having penetrated several inches in all cases. In his opinion she could never have survived the attack not even for a few minutes, any one of the chest wounds being mortal. He added, almost as a footnote, that the dinner knife found by the body was also most certainly not the murder weapon, in fact, forensic examination had showed it had never even been used in the killing.

From the moment of Ellen's disappearance until the discovery of her body, Colour Sergeant Major Hepburn remained strangely silent. There can be absolutely no doubt he knew she had never returned to camp. He was in the officers' mess on several occasions when her failure to report back had been discussed. But during those same conversations, when he could so easily have admitted his involvement in her life, he said nothing. Neither did he join the search party sent out on the Monday afternoon. That silence he maintained until after Ellen's body had been found and identified. Only then did he volunteer a statement to his commanding officer, no doubt well aware as he did so, that his name had already been mentioned to police. The woman who had first reported Ellen's failure to return, a Miss Hickson, the Corps administrator, had also given his name as the man she had intended to meet on the Friday evening. Common sense must have told him that it were better he admit his association with the dead girl, regardless of how tenuous, than have police discover it. So, at 4.45 pm, some hour or so after Ellen had been found in the wood, Hepburn walked into the office of Camp Commander, Lieutenant Colonel Phillips, and declared his interest:

> *On the evening of 8 May I attended a dance held at Haynes Park Camp, where my partner for most of the evening was the deceased. During the evening she said there was a lorry leaving the camp next day between 3.30 pm and 5 pm, and mentioned that she intended to accompany same and asked me to go too. I promised to do so. Between the hour of 3.30 pm and 4 pm on 9 May I left the demobilisation hut for my quarters and on the way passed deceased, whom I informed I would catch up by proceeding on the lorry, which had not then arrived. She agreed saying she would walk on. At 5 pm the lorry left with me, and I kept a sharp look out all the way to Bedford, expecting to see deceased. As I did not see her I went to the river alone . . .*

Within hours of making this statement, he was arrested and taken by car to Bedford police station. Unsurprisingly, he was the only suspect in the case. Nothing had been found at the murder scene to show conclusively that someone other than Hepburn had carried out the killing, so it seemed reasonable to assume that the man who had remained so silent throughout the weekend, had done so for good reason. That reason being that in a frenzied and probably unprovoked attack, he had stabbed Ellen Rault to death, supposition of course, but not entirely without foundation.

There were inconsistencies in Hepburn's brief statement, which police were quick to seize upon. Unbeknown to the sergeant major, when he stood in front of his commanding officer to make that statement, they already had a pretty good idea of time of death. Calculated from the evidence of others, it suggested she had died within minutes of having left the camp, which by Hepburn's own admission, made him possibly the last to see her alive.

Firstly there was the evidence of Sarah Stokes. A school teacher at Haynes Infant School, she knew Ellen by sight and on the evening of her murder had seen her sitting with her back against a tree reading a book, just outside the camp gates at around four o'clock. Then there was sixteen-year-old Miss Harling, a passenger in a pony and trap. She passed the same

Bedford Boys Modern School c1920. Author's collection

spot fifteen minutes later, having travelled from Bedford to
Haynes, and saw no one; her evidence was corroborated by two
young women cyclists who had ridden from the top of Wilstead
Woods. They too told police they had not passed or seen Ellen
on the Bedford road. Finally, there was the testimony of Private
Rush. He walked out through the camp gates at around a
quarter past four that evening. He confirmed having been
passed by the pony and Trap, and added that some fifteen or
so yards from the camp's main gates he had seen two schoolboys pick up what he believed had been a book. The book was
eventually traced and Bedford Modern schoolboy, John Bray,
later took police to a spot opposite the murder site. The book
was one of poetry and had belonged to Ellen Rault.

So, what all that meant was that Ellen had almost certainly
met her killer within minutes of leaving the camp, probably at
some time between 3.45 pm and 4.15 pm. Initially not damning
for Hepburn, as he had confirmed meeting Ellen between 3 30
pm and 4 pm. But for police that was too vague. With witness
evidence placing her outside the camp at four o'clock, but no
sightings after that time, they wanted Hepburn to be more
precise. When he appeared unable to comply they checked his
movements inside the camp. That quickly revealed he had left

the demobilisation hut, where he had been on duty throughout the Friday afternoon, at four o'clock. Sergeant George Smith, who had worked alongside him that day, recalled the two men had left the hut to go for tea at a few minutes to four. But that Hepburn had not gone to the mess hall and did not return to the hut.

Further enquiries had also revealed that the lorry that had carried him to Bedford had actually left the Camp at 4.40 pm, not 5 pm as Hepburn had stated. The driver was able to be precise simply because upon their arrival at the town, Sanderson's Works were turning out and they did not stop work until 5 pm.

To the police all this conflicting evidence meant Hepburn had lied. He could not possibly have met Ellen until four o'clock because that had been his earliest opportunity. Also, she had to have died within minutes of that meeting, as shown by the various witness accounts. Furthermore, he had a forty-minute window of opportunity to commit the murder, a period of time he failed to account for, the time between that meeting and the lorry leaving the camp. As the cell door closed behind

The church at Haynes where Ellen was buried with full military honours. The author

him that Monday night it all looked bleak for the sergeant major.

The inquest opened in the cadet's mess hall at Haynes Camp on Wednesday 13 May 1919. The hearing lasted for four days and heard evidence from thirty witnesses. Unfortunately for the police, most of that evidence was both conflicting and confused. What they believed was a clear body of evidence in support of their contention that they had caught Ellen Rault's killer fell apart in the courtroom, whilst that surrounding Ellen's last moments was reasonably solid, and the timeline of events they had created accurate, the same could not be said of that intended to prove Hepburn's guilt. Here, the testimony produced was at best vague and at worst muddled.

Police needed to build on their contention that not only had he lied but also that he had engineered the opportunity to carry out the killing. But when the various army personnel gave their evidence, it rapidly became clear that there were serious anomalies. Key to the police case was being able to show that Hepburn had never returned to the demob hut after 4 pm. But three witnesses all gave conflicting accounts, suggesting that quite possibly he had returned to the hut until around the time of the lorry's departure for Bedford. Also, by the final day of the hearing, police had been told that examination of all the sergeant's clothing had revealed no bloodstaining. Neither had traces of blood been found on his army knife.

In his summing up to the jury the coroner, having addressed the inconsistencies told the jury that despite what they had heard there was still a case to answer:

> They had evidence that there was no one in the road except this girl. Who would be most likely to know the habits of the camp? It must have been some soldier, probably a soldier who knew her. There was one soldier whose name was constantly brought up throughout this case, day after day, and there was no other name except that of Sergeant Major Hepburn, which was mentioned in connexion with this girl at all. Almost at the outset of the inquiry it was remarked that Hepburn had an appointment with the girl at 3.30 that afternoon. You have heard Hepburn in his written statement . . . and you know from the evidence that during the time the girl was missing on the Friday afternoon until after the body was found, no report was made by Hepburn to anyone in authority that he had an appointment with the girl and she hadn't come, and he wondered what had become of her. Was it not a reasonable inference to think . . . if she didn't keep the

appointment and was reported missing would not the average man say. "It is very curious. I had better make some enquiries and say I had an appointment with her" . . .

The jury did not share the same concerns and instead of the expected verdict of murder against Hepburn they returned an open verdict. For the Sergeant Major it was a cause for celebration. If the coroner's court was unable to agree that he had murdered Ellen Rault then what chance the magistrates' court? He had good reason to be optimistic. When the court finally sat on 5 June all charges against him were dropped without any evidence being heard. Colour Sergeant Major Hepburn was then formally discharged.

Did he kill her? Who now knows? Certainly there was enough circumstantial evidence to suggest that he did, but there was absolutely nothing to either place him at the scene or show that he possessed the murder weapon. The only certain fact is that, as the coroner pointed out, she knew her killer, and probably did die within minutes of leaving the camp. The killer was lucky. As the evidence shows, enough people were around that afternoon but not at the crucial time!

CHAPTER 11

The Blunham Mystery

The Suspicious Deaths of Mr & Mrs Marshall Blunham, 1929

All the evidence pointed toward the car having somehow left the road, hit the telegraph pole and burst into flames.

When coal-man Alfred Timms and his good friend Frank Goodwin saw smoke billowing from a stationary car they immediately ran toward it, to extinguish the fire. The car, a 1924 Buick, was parked on the grass verge just in front of a telegraph pole, which it appeared to have collided with, on Ridge Road, Blunham, and the fire was fierce. So fierce in fact that by the time the two men reached it there was absolutely nothing they could do. Goodwin, home on leave from the Grenadier Guards and

Blunham village today. The author

St George's Road, Bedford today. The author

probably the fitter of the two, made several attempts to reach the driver's door; each attempt beaten back by the intense heat until exhaustion forced him to quit. At that point, as the windows shattered from the heat, Timms dragged him back to the other side of the road. From there, as the wind whipped the flames into a frenzy, the men watched in stunned silence, their attention gripped by the double silhouette of the driver and his passenger engulfed in fire; all to well aware nothing could be done to save their lives. So began the Blunham mystery.

The fire, which had lasted in all about an hour, was finally extinguished by the local fire brigade at around midnight. Inside the burnt out wreck of the car when they were finally able to examine it, police found two bodies, a man and a woman. Both were still in their seats at the front though the woman had died with her head on the man's shoulder. Initial conclusions suggested the deaths were accidental. All the early evidence pointed toward the car having somehow left the road, hit the telegraph pole and burst into flames. The occupants, quite possibly concussed, had probably died as a result of smoke inhalation.

By dawn on the following day, 10 September 1929, police had identified the dead couple as Lindsay Marshall and his wife, Eva. The car's make had been distinctive and the licence plate known to local police. Well-known in the area, the Marshalls had farmed much of the land around Blunham for years from their home at South Mills Farm. After interviewing the housemaid, Edith Norman, they learned that the couple had left the farm at around a quarter to eight the previous night, simply to take a drive in the car, apparently something the two of them did regularly. But police were sceptical; by the time they had left the farm it was dark – to their minds too dark for a bit of pointless driving. Their scepticism was well founded. By late that same day they had learned that within fifteen minutes of leaving the farm the couple were in Bedford. There they had called on family friend John Mackelvie. They stayed at his house on St George's Road for over an hour. As they left they made an arrangement for his daughter to stay over at the farm on the following Tuesday (14 September). According to Mr MacKelvie, the Marshalls were intending to drive straight back to Blunham and were in high spirits when they set off. But despite further rigorous enquiries it seemed the Marshall's car then disappeared for some two hours, finally surfacing ablaze in Blunham at 11pm. As police towed the car away that night they were reasonably satisfied the whole episode had been one tragic accident. Then came the gun.

In a seemingly totally unrelated incident three boys reported finding a revolver in the river under the bridge at Great Barford. It appeared that as police were leaving Blunham on the Friday night twenty-four hours after the car blaze, in nearby Great Barford a group of schoolboys had just begun fishing. The spot they had chosen was the one that had proved productive throughout the week, a stretch of shallow water on the Willington side of Barford Bridge. But this time as they cast off one of them spotted an object just below the waters surface that glinted in the evening sunlight. When he pulled it to the bank he found himself holding a handgun with five of its six chambers still loaded. On the following morning (Saturday 11 September) it was handed over to Bedford police.

They followed normal procedures and two days later had identified the gun's owner. It was Lindsay Marshall. At that point the notion of a tragic accident was dropped in favour of something far more sinister, though just how sinister police at that point were still uncertain. But enquiries in Bedford later revealed that Lindsay Marshall had purchased the revolver

The bridge at Great Barford viewed from the Willington side. The author

from a Bedford gunsmith. He had applied for a gun licence on 17 July, some three weeks earlier. The licence had been granted by 26 August and he made his purchase on 6 September, only three days before his death. Even more strange was the fact that at the time of the purchase he also bought fifty rounds of ammunition, but none of it fit the revolver. When police made a search of the farm and its outbuildings they discovered, rather bizarrely, that instead of returning the faulty ammunition to the shop, he had carefully filed down the bullets until they had fit the chamber. Those found inside the revolver after its discovery showed clear signs of having undergone this process, but what did it all mean?

Police having reassessed their original conclusions surrounding the car fire began to believe that the gun had somehow played a role in the Marshall's deaths and began a new search for clues. A car expert, familiar with the make and model, was brought in from General Motors in order to better understand how the fire started. A more thorough forensic examination was also made of the car debris in a search for clues that could indicate violence and a full post-mortem was ordered on the two bodies. Then came the poison.

Whilst all this was ongoing, Lloyds the chemist rang police to say they had a record of Lindsay Marshall having bought prussic acid in August. The reason he had given for the purchase was that he wanted to poison his cowman's dog. Why he wanted to do so was never elaborated upon. But the chemist did provide him with one ounce in a small bottle. A second detailed search of the farm failed to discover the bottles whereabouts and the cowman confirmed that it had never been used to kill his dog. For Inspector Goodwin, who was handling the case, it was just another piece of the jigsaw puzzle that seemed to be slowly unravelling about him. But it was about to get worse.

When Frederick Wright, the technical expert sent in from General Motors, handed in his report the case took yet another twist. The results of his extremely thorough examination revealed that the car had never been in collision with the telegraph pole. Far from it, in fact the dent on the front mudguard of the car had been made elsewhere and had absolutely nothing to do with the blaze. The seat of the fire, he had discovered, had begun behind the car's occupants. Traces of petrol were still to be found in the wreckage, not just around the engine compartment but also on the seats. It had been this, insisted Mr Wright, which had caused such a fierce blaze. Without the addition of an accelerant, the velour fabric used for the car's upholstery would never have ignited. But this was not to be the final piece of the puzzle, that came in the shape of a young woman named Florence Hull.

According to her statement, made shortly after the car expert had delivered his verdict, she had heard a gunshot on the night the Marshall's car caught fire. What's more, that shot came from Barford Bridge and the sound was definitely that of a hand gun as distinct from that of a shotgun. Living on a farm, she was well qualified to recognise the difference between the two weapons. She was also close enough to be able to be reasonably certain as to the direction of the sound. The Hull family owned Bridge Farm, so named because it was within sight of the bridge across the river at Great Barford. What was unusual about her evidence was that she was also precise as to the timing of the shot. The gun was fired, she insisted, at precisely twenty-three minutes to eleven at night. She claimed it had frightened her mother, that was why they had noted the time, and it had been followed by the sound of a car engine starting then driving off.

From all this evidence police then began to formulate the

theory that perhaps Lindsay Marshall had shot his wife, thrown the gun into the river, driven to Blunham, deliberately damaged his car, parked off the road, poisoned himself, then set the Buick alight. Certainly plausible, but could it have happened that way? If it did then police believed the post-mortem results would prove the theory. Unfortunately, when they did come they were far from conclusive. Absolutely nothing was found on the bodies to suggest gunshot wounds, no entry or exit wound on Eva Marshall and no poison residue. Although the pathologist did point out that the remains were so badly burnt that conclusive evidence one way or the other was never going to be obtained. At that point they shifted their search for clues back to the car. If, as they had postulated, a gun had been fired at Mrs Marshall would not the bullet, if not in the body be in the car? Equally so, if prussic acid had been used where was the empty bottle? Prussic acid is a cyanide poison, it kills within minutes and if Lindsay Marshall drank the ounce he had bought from Lloyds he must have done so whilst the car was parked. That meant, as police well knew, that the bottle had to have stayed inside the car. Nothing was found.

Blunham Cemetery where it is thought the Marshalls were buried. Author's collection

Somewhat bewildered by the lack of supportive evidence, police nevertheless continued with their theory that what they had found on the 9 September was murder and suicide. When the inquest finally got under way on 25 September 1929, before Bedford coroner Gregory Whyley, they argued there was no other logical explanation. Every indication was, they told the jury, that Lindsay Marshall had planned, not only the double killing, but also to confound police investigations, which he knew would follow, by deliberately hiding or concealing the relevant evidence. They told the court that had he thrown the revolver on the other side of the bridge it would have fallen into deep water and probably never been found. The likelihood was that had that been the case then the conclusion drawn would have been one of accidental death, which they believed was Lindsay Marshall's intended verdict. The discovery of the gun was the single most important piece of evidence. Inspector Goodwin told the court that accidental death was impossible to believe once police had the weapon in their hands. The ammunition was so distinctive that it precluded any third party involvement. Add to that the sound of the gunshot followed by a car moving away, the purchase of poison, the purposeful placing of the car in front of the telegraph pole, the damaged front mudguard meant to mislead, and the petrol used as an accelerant. Taken together, they clearly show a level of premeditation that is almost unimaginable.

It all made sense but the coroner wanted to know, if all this had been true, then what was the motive? To that end he called a number a witnesses designed to shed light on both the character of the Marshalls and their financial state, the argument being that if the police theory were correct then there had to have been a reason behind all the meticulous planning. Unfortunately, by the close of the second day, the court had heard nothing to support police conclusions. Numerous witnesses were able to testify to the fact that the Marshall's marriage was sound. The couple were rarely out of each other's company and arguments almost non-existent. Furthermore, their diaries suggested a deal of planning for the short-term future, and those employed by the farm had noticed no discernable outward change in their behaviour. Barclay's Bank told the hearing that the farmer's debts, some £14,000, were not unusual and were all underwritten. Mr Marshall had been astute enough to lodge sureties with the bank, including a significant life insurance policy, for all his borrowings, which meant the debts were essentially, risk free. The farm, they told the coroner, was an extremely profitable business producing a high annual yield. The annual accounts supported that and showed healthy profits against the last few years. In their opinion Mr Marshall had no financial concerns. The view was supported by other small creditors, none of who showed the slightest concern for the levels of debt incurred against them. In fact the highest small trader debt was only £250, hardly an amount worth a life.

So, as the coroner drew the hearing to a close at the end of the third and final day, the court were not a deal further forward. In his closing speech to the jury he told them there were only two possible outcomes to the inquest. The first was accidental death and the second was murder and suicide. An open verdict could not be given simply because the discovery of the revolver and its ownership were clear indicators that no other person had been involved in the two deaths. He favoured the murder and suicide verdict simply because there were too many inconsistencies in the arguments supporting accidental fire. He told the jurors he accepted the police theory that the whole tragic event appeared to have been staged. But, he added, no motive had been found, which would always create an element of doubt. It was clear from the evidence, he went on, that Lindsay Marshall appeared to have absolutely no need to take his life but having decided to do so, for whatever reason, he must have felt the need for subterfuge. For that there could only be one explanation, the life policy held by the bank. Accidental death was therefore a verdict he needed from the inquest, which he knew must follow the cars discovery if the insurance company were to pay his debtors. But that, he told the jury, cannot be.

After an adjournment of fifteen minutes the jury agreed with coroner Whyley and brought a verdict of murder and suicide. Was it fair? In the circumstances yes it was, but did it reflect all the evidence? Of course it did not, which is why the case remains the mystery it has become.

CHAPTER 12

A Sad Case of Insanity

The Killing of Arthur Morley
Bedford, 1942

He immediately admitted his guilt . . .

rthur Luddington had been an angry man for much of his life, just why had always remained a mystery. Arthur never sought medical help. Instead, he took out his anger on his wife and son, Kenneth. When in one of his tempers he would instantly fly into a rage, tear at his hair, hurl pots at the wall and grab either of them by the throat. At those times he would instantly turn from being mild mannered, almost placid, to a raging maniac intent on violence, a Jekyll and Hyde character his family found almost impossible to live with. But as his son Kenneth grew, so did his resistance. He began to harbour resentment, a deep-seated bitterness, that in turn created the same flash of anger that inhabited his father's head. By the time he had reached his twenties he was big enough and strong enough to fight back. Only a grudging respect for his father's position in the house held him back. But by the summer of 1942 that resistance was slowly being eaten away.

Twenty-six-years-old by that time, still living with his parents on Iddesleigh Road, Bedford, he worked nearby as a turner. At the outbreak of war, rejected by the Army, he had joined the Home Guard. That meant he was working shifts at the factory and giving up his free time to train in the local militia. This in turn added a pressure to his daily life that he was totally unaccustomed to and on top of all that his teeth were rotten and a source of constant pain. Taken separately these stresses were all easily manageable, but taken as a whole they created in Kenneth Luddington something akin to a walking time bomb. Something his father, to his great detriment, never noticed. It was to cost him dear.

At eleven thirty on the morning of 5 July, after working on

St Peter's Street, Bedford c1920. Author's collection

his allotment since breakfast, Arthur Luddington walked into the kitchen carrying an armful of vegetables. Toiling in the soil for several hours had done little to lift his spirits. He was vexed, a little tetchy and snapped at his wife. When Kenneth followed him in some minutes later he turned on him angrily and ordered him out of the house. There was no reason to do so, but Kenneth had endured these temper tantrums so many times that he simply turned on his heels and left. He went straight to the nearest pub.

At just after two o'clock in the afternoon he returned to the house clutching a bottle of stout for his mother. The atmosphere was calmer; his father had taken off his boots and was sat in his usual chair in the dining room whilst his mother cooked dinner. Kenneth ignored her, brushed past, went straight up to his father and, without speaking, simply swung the bottle of stout at him. The bottle hit him squarely in the face. Kenneth then struck out a second time. As his father slipped into unconsciousness he put the bottle on the floor, seized the rifle he shouldered with the Home Guard, and using the butt end of it smashed his father's head to pulp. At that point his mother ran out into the street to fetch help. As she ran screaming through the kitchen Kenneth then fetched a razor and brutally hacked at his father until he was dead. He then went and stood outside to wait for the police.

They arrived at just after half-past two. Kenneth was still calm, almost pleased with himself. He immediately admitted his guilt and offered to show them the body:

It's murder. Would you like to see him?

They followed him into the house and stated later that when they had viewed the body of Arthur Luddington he was so disfigured as to be barely recognisable. Kenneth was arrested, taken to Bedford police station and later that same day charged with murder. From that point on began the debate as to whether Kenneth Luddington had been insane when he had carried out the killing.

When he took his place in the dock before the Hon Sir Geoffrey Lawrence on 11 October 1942 that debate had still not been resolved. Under advice, he pleaded not guilty and his barrister, Mr Richard O'Sullivan, in his address to the jury submitted that at the time the killing was done Luddington was suffering from insanity in the legal sense, meaning, of course, that he had no real knowledge of what he was doing:

Iddesleigh Road, Bedford today. The author

The savagery of it was committed by a man who was out of his mind – who was, if you will, beside himself. I ask you to say in your judgement that a fair and proper inference to draw is that he was out of his mind.

Success in his plea depended solely on the opinion of doctors and there he found his assertion difficult to prove.

Dr Oliver, who had spent time with Luddington in Bedford Prison, told the court that he had thoroughly examined him during his incarceration. He added that at no time had he denied his involvement; on the contrary, he appeared to demonstrate a very accurate memory of events in the house on the day of the killing. Nothing, he added, in either his demeanour or general well being indicated a preponderance to madness. As far as the prison doctor was concerned, Kenneth Luddington was quite sane. This opinion was then upheld by the family doctor, John Boyd. He told the court that although he had only known Luddington since 1941, in that short time he had never witnessed behaviour, which he would have classed as psychotic.

But those findings were strongly contested by Dr Henry Yellowlees, a Harley Street, psychiatrist. In his testimony to the court he stated that in his opinion Luddington suffered from a slowly developing and insidious mental disease, known as paranoid schizophrenia, or split-mind. That meant he would not have known what he was doing when he attacked his father. Furthermore, he insisted, when examined in prison during the first week of October he had demonstrated this in various ways, including possible hereditary tendencies. His father was thought to have shown clear signs of mental illness. It was therefore perfectly reasonable to assume, he told the judge, that Kenneth had inherited a similar deficiency. There could be no doubt, he insisted, that the prisoner had been insane when he struck the fatal blows.

It was left to the judge's summing up at the end of the short trial to clarify the key points to the jury. He, it seemed, was of the opinion that Luddington had not demonstrated sufficient psychotic tendencies to support the notion that he had been quite mad when he picked up the rifle, or the bottle and finally the razor, though he did concede that the Harley Street doctor was a recognised authority within the field of mental health. But he was less than impressed with the London doctor's theory of inherited madness. Quite rightly, he pointed out that no evidence had been brought to court that would support the notion that the son had inherited schizophrenia from the father:

. . . you have to consider whether the medical evidence applied to the prisoner, proved that his reason was affected by a disease of the mind so that at the time of the act he either did not know what he was doing or did not know he was doing wrong . . .

After an adjournment of one hour and twenty minutes the jury returned to court unable to reach a decision. After some discussion with the judge they were sent back to the jury room to reconsider and thirty-five minutes later came back to court with a guilty, but insane, verdict. Kenneth Luddington was sent to a secure mental asylum.

CHAPTER 13

The High Price of Fruit

The Shooting of Thomas Astle
Kempston, 1942

The two cannoned into each other beside a drainage ditch . . .

Kempston shopkeeper, Ernest Robinson, had spent much of his life in or around Bedford. Well known locally, he had set aside time each and every week to help those less fortunate, something he considered his duty and a duty he never shirked. Borne of his belief in the church, he had become a lay preacher in the early 1930s; he never saw his charity work as onerous, rather as a reward. Kempston and its people had been good to him over the years

Outskirts of Bedford as it looked c1940. Author's collection

and as he grew older he wanted to divert some of his energies back into the community. He enjoyed the work, believed whole heartedly in the church and all its workings, and felt he had earned the right to do what he could for people he felt to be less fortunate than himself. If he had any vice it was the cultivation of his precious fruit trees, of which he had a number.

By August of 1942 those trees were heavy with their summer crop. The government had been urging people to grow their own food, dig up their lawns, their village greens, wasteland, in short any community space that could support a crop. Food was in short supply. Imports were severely curtailed. Merchant shipping had been badly hit by the German U boats. The war in the Atlantic was at its height and thousands of tons of food products and other consumables had already been lost to the submarine packs, not to mention sailor's lives. So, Ernest, by this time sixty-seven years old, wanted to do his bit. The fruit would be put to good use, some he would sell, some he would eat and some he would give away – provided he could prevent pilfering.

Bedford in 1942, like most towns and cities up and down the UK, was full of service personnel. Some just passing through, others stationed nearby, all strangers in a strange place. In many ways local communities had changed out of all recognition. Faces no one knew were mixing with those who had spent the whole of their life in the same place. There was a migration of sorts caused by the military who by necessity had been forced to move men, and women, around the country into the various army camps that had sprung up to house them. In turn that meant more and more anonymous people and some of those people unscrupulous enough to steal from the very communities into which they had been brought. Ernest could certainly testify to that. Since mid-July he had noticed his fruit crop disappearing, and the quantities were too large to have been to local schoolboy raids. So, with the help of a neighbour, he resolved to stop the thieving. Between the two of them they would mount guard.

All went well until the early hours of Tuesday 18 August. At around midnight Ernest, sneaking around the fields perimeter armed with an old shotgun, saw movement amongst the fruit trees. He shouted out an alarm and ran toward the silhouette of a man. At his age his legs were never going to carry him far and had the man run off in the opposite direction all would probably have turned out well. But the man was unfamiliar with his surroundings and, disorientated by the dark, panicked. The two

Kempston High Street today. Author's collection

cannoned into each other beside a drainage ditch that ran alongside the field. There was a brief scuffle, both men then fell into the shallow water, the gun went off and the stranger stopped moving. By the time Ernest had extracted himself he realised the dead man was a soldier.

Police arrived at the scene at around one o'clock in the morning. The body, later identified as Lance Corporal Thomas Astle, lay face down. The soldier wore full battledress and had been shot in the chest. According to doctor John Tree who examined the corpse, the shot had killed him instantly and caused massive internal damage to the heart, lungs and right shoulder. Ernest, distraught by what had happened, denied having intentionally fired the gun. In his statement to police he insisted the weapon had discharged accidentally during the brief struggle in the ditch. According to the old man he had never intended to use the shotgun at all. It was merely for show, intended only to scare away thieves. What he could not explain was why he had loaded it in the first place. Police charged him with murder and he was taken to Bedford police station.

There he stayed until later that same day when he made his

Bedford Town c1920. Author's collection

first appearance in Bedford magistrates' court. He had nothing to add to the statement he had made immediately after his arrest and requested that he be allowed bail. It was refused despite Ernest's good reputation, age and Christian leanings, on the grounds that he had been charged with a capital offence. There was no doubting the court's view that despite his plea that it had been accidental they considered the shot had been fired 'with deliberate intent'. Ernest was taken to Bedford Prison and there he stayed until 11 October.

But during his incarceration a full post-mortem revealed that the court had been wrong. The gunshot wound and powder burns to Thomas Astle's uniform clearly indicated that when the gun had been fired the two men had been locked together. In the police reconstruction the gun was probably between the pair as they wrestled in the drainage ditch. This meant Ernest had no opportunity to aim the weapon. Therefore, premeditation was discounted. According to the pathologist, in order to have received the type of wound Astle had suffered there could have been no intention to kill, more an accidental firing that had caught the young soldier as he tried to break free of Ernest Robinson's grip.

HEAVY CALENDAR AT ASSIZES

Bedford Murder Case: Accused Found Guilty but Insane

KEMPSTON SHOPKEEPER ACQUITTED

When Bedfordshire Autumn Assizes opened last Friday morning, there was a long list of criminal cases, including two capital charges, before the Judge (the Hon. Sir Geoffrey Lawrence, Kt., D.S.O.). It was, in fact, the heaviest calendar in recent years, and the most serious for many years. Altogether fifteen men, including six Service men, were down to be tried on eighteen charges. When the Assizes concluded on Monday evening there were still three charges of bribery against two men to be heard, and these cases have been transferred to the Nottinghamshire Assizes next month. Two courts were held on Friday, the ten cases in the second court being heard by the Commissioner of Assize (Mr. P. E. Sandlands, K.C.). In the first court two men appeared on murder charges, and one on a manslaughter charge. The hearing of the first of these cases started on Friday morning, and the last concluded on Monday evening. Public interest in the Assizes was unusually high, and there were crowded courts.

The Bedford Times *headline announcing Robinson's acquittal in October 1942.* The *Bedford Times*

So, when he took his place in the dock in Bedford's court-house, his defence counsel immediately applied for the charge of murder to be dropped. They argued that in light of the evidence the charge had no substance to it and must fail. The judge agreed and asked the prosecution if they wished to proceed on the grounds of manslaughter, which he felt was the only avenue available to them. They declined, so, turning to the jury he told them the case was unsafe:

Having regard to the view I have indicated it would be very unsafe for a conviction to be recorded against this man. The prosecution propose to offer no evidence and it is your duty to find the prisoner not guilty.

Ernest returned to his business and his fruit trees though this time without the use of a gun.

CHAPTER 14

The Body in the Sack Murder

The Death of Irene Manton
Luton, 1943

. . . he placed the body in a wheelbarrow . . . and dropped it into the river.

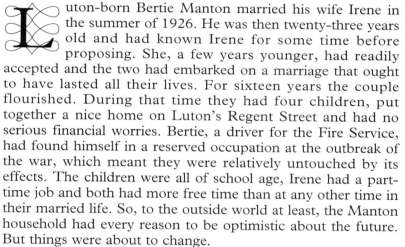 uton-born Bertie Manton married his wife Irene in the summer of 1926. He was then twenty-three years old and had known Irene for some time before proposing. She, a few years younger, had readily accepted and the two had embarked on a marriage that ought to have lasted all their lives. For sixteen years the couple flourished. During that time they had four children, put together a nice home on Luton's Regent Street and had no serious financial worries. Bertie, a driver for the Fire Service, had found himself in a reserved occupation at the outbreak of the war, which meant they were relatively untouched by its effects. The children were all of school age, Irene had a part-time job and both had more free time than at any other time in their married life. So, to the outside world at least, the Manton household had every reason to be optimistic about the future. But things were about to change.

By spring, 1942, as the victorious Japanese army seized Singapore and the battered American navy prepared to fight the battle of Midway, Irene decided to change her job. She wanted more money, more friends, and more freedom. In short she wanted to live life at a faster pace. The war had given her a sense of urgency, the same kind of urgency she saw in the faces of the servicemen that filled the town at night. Outside her home a war was being fought, a struggle for life and death. She saw it every day in the skies above her head, heard it every night on the radio, and read it every morning in her newspaper. For her it was no time to be a homemaker, housewife, mother, it was a time to be alive and that cost more financially than her marriage could provide. So, she put a stop to her part-time

Regent Street, Luton today. The author

work and began on the day shift at a nearby tobacco factory. The work was repetitive, at times boring but always lucrative. There she mixed with women of her own age alongside those from a younger generation she hardly knew and found she loved every minute of it. Inevitably, nights out became a regular ·feature of her week, most spent in nearby pubs and clubs, sometimes straight after work, other times weekends or early afternoons, depending on her shift patterns. There her social circle widened, as she had intended it would, her drinking partners more of a sexual mix, which she enjoyed hugely because it gave her the freedom to enjoy male company away from the watchful eye of her husband. In turn that meant her alcohol consumption increased, though not beyond the bounds of social acceptance, just enough to aid her new, more forceful character to rise to the surface; something Bertie found harder and harder to handle.

Back home it is fair to say that he extended few courtesies to her newfound friends whenever they came to call, instead, refusing to acknowledge them whenever he could, laying the blame for his changed circumstances squarely at their door.

Bad company, as he termed them whenever he and Irene argued, and throughout 1942 those arguments grew evermore vicious and vitriolic. Irene's departure from the housewife ways he had grown used to, and to a large extent rely upon, had brought about a major shift in how the home was run. She no longer had the same level of day-to-day involvement with the children as she once had. That had fallen more to Bertie, as had some of the normal household chores like cooking and cleaning, though this had not necessarily come about solely as a result of her new found social life. Shift work alone would have had an inevitable knock-on effect within their relationship. What caused its impact to be more pronounced than perhaps it ought was Irene's constant unreliability. To Bertie, by autumn of that year her behaviour had become totally unacceptable. By this time Irene's drinking after work had evolved into more than just an hour or two socialising with work colleagues. Arriving home well after eleven o'clock at night had by then become the norm. She could no longer be relied upon to be sober, therefore unlikely to be able to take charge of the children if she were needed. At least that was how he saw it and so, on 21 November 1942, after yet another acrimonious row over her drinking, they agreed to split. Irene returned to her mother's house on Church Street, Luton. Bertie stayed in the family home and looked after the children.

Church Street, Luton today. The author

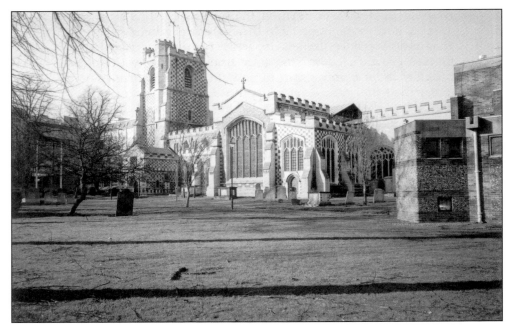

St Mary's church, Luton. The author

For four months life was relatively trouble free. The children had regular access to their mother whilst living with their father and seemed to accept the arrangement. Irene had free access to her new friends whenever she wanted outside stimulus without the need to apologise each time she returned at night. But Bertie still hankered after the old life, the one he felt he had lost to the war. Because of this, every time the two of them met he urged her to return, go back home, and rekindle their marriage. Initially, Irene resisted, there were advantages to her single life, advantages she was reluctant to give up. But Bertie was a persuasive man and in March 1943, after weeks of badgering, he finally convinced her that between them they could, if they worked hard enough, pick up the threads of their marriage and start again. Or at least that was how it appeared to the outside world. Whether she did actually buy into his version of wedded bliss and that was why she chose to return is debatable. Quite possibly it was because she missed her children and there were still financial needs for both of them. Either way she was back at the family home by mid-March and for some few weeks all appeared to be going well. But by May the old trouble had resurfaced. Irene was back on the town and when Bertie discovered she had been going to dances with serving soldiers they split a second time. The second separation, however, was short, three weeks only, mainly because Irene decided to escape her marriage at the same time as her sister and their mother only had room for one of them. As Irene had already taken advantage weeks earlier it fell to her to make the magnanimous gesture and so she returned home. The move was to prove disastrous for both of them.

Again, initially all went well, so well that in August 1943 Irene announced that she was pregnant. Bertie was ecstatic and the two of them appeared to settle down to enjoy the summer. But all was far from being well. Beneath this facade of family unity lay a still unresolved anger and whenever it resurfaced they fought. The arguments were often petty in nature, some times short-lived, rarely violent – but enough to cause a sense of rancour and bitterness that began to permeate the relationship to such an extent that any sense of amity was eventually totally destroyed.

Toward the end of the summer Bertie, despite Irene's protestations, took on a part-time, odd job role at the nearby *Plume of Feathers* pub. Unconvinced by Bertie's argument that they needed the money, she believed he had an ulterior motive for being around the bar each night, and it was not the beer. Leastways, that was how Bertie chose to interpret her objection, though whether she was jealous of some local barmaid, as he liked to believe, is debateable. Either way, it was undoubtedly the source of a number of acrimonious arguments throughout the autumn of 1943, culminating in the fight five weeks before Christmas that cost her her life.

On 18 November of that year, as had been the practice throughout their marriage, they prepared lunch for the children as usual. At around one o'clock in the afternoon the whole family sat down to eat. The meal went off without a hitch and at just after two o'clock the children all left the house, some to return to school, some to return to their jobs. Bertie helped Irene clear away the dishes then washed up for her as she sat by the fire. When everything was back in its place he made a pot of tea, poured out two cups, gave one to Irene and went and sat opposite her with the other. It had been an argument-free day and probably would have remained so had he not then mentioned his planned visit to the pub. Like throwing oil on a fire, Irene went ballistic, shouting abuse at him from the other side of the room, calling him names and eventually, perhaps out of frustration, grabbing her cup and hurling its contents in his face. Bertie, with no time to react, was temporarily blinded, the hot tea also burned him and, as he pushed himself to his feet, he was suddenly knocked backwards as Irene rushed at him. The two of them fought in the fireside chair until Bertie, in a fit of anger grabbed her by the neck to push her back. Then, reaching down with his right hand he grabbed a hold of a small wooden stool and smashed it into the side of her head twice. Irene was almost dead when her body hit the floor.

For a long time Bertie did nothing but cry. Then he knelt beside Irene's body, which was saturated in blood, and tried to make sense of what he had just done. He knew there was no going back. Irene was never going to recover. Question was, did he notify the police? Did he admit what he had done? confess and probably go to the gallows? Or did he hide the body, deny murder and hope to stay free? He chose the latter. In the cellar he remembered there were four old sacks and a ball of string. He ran down and fetched them then, slicing open the empty sacking he stripped Irene of her clothes, removed her false teeth then wrapped her in the hessian and tied it in place. The body he then hid until nightfall. As the children arrived home he gave them each money and sent them back out. When he thought the streets were quiet enough he placed the body in a wheel-barrow, pushed it to Osborne Road Bridge and dropped it into the river. The obvious intention being that the body would sink or be carried far enough down river for it to disappear forever,

Osborne Road, Luton. The author

but probably it was too dark to be certain. When he arrived back home he then burnt all Irene's clothes on the fire, along with her dentures and told the children later that she had gone to stay with their grandma. They never questioned it. But Bertie had been extremely careless, he ought to have known that bodies rarely sink unless they have been well weighted and this one had not been. Irene's body resurfaced twenty-four hours later and was found by two council workman only yards from where he had left it.

But he still had one advantage. For the police, identity was to prove a major obstacle to solving her death. Removing her clothing, jewellery and particularly the false teeth had given to Irene an anonymity he could never have hoped for. So, whilst the newspaper headlines called for public help in identifying the body in the sack, he went to London on three separate days, each one week apart, and posted letters purporting to be from Irene, back to her mother in Luton. Bizarrely, the subterfuge worked, but police were not about to allow their enquiries to be so easily thwarted. In a bold step they had photographers make up a short film that showed Irene's face. This they inserted into cinema programming, which was then shown to audiences as they watched newsreel footage from the various battlefronts. Inevitably, it led them to Regent Street and on the 22 February 1944 Bertie Manton was finally arrested.

Initially, he denied that the body found in the river was Irene, citing the forged letters to her mother, which he claimed to have seen, as evidence that she was still alive and well somewhere in London. By way of corroboration he even added that he had seen her at Luton Market in December though could not be certain as to the date. But by this time handwriting experts had already uncovered the deception and police knew he had also travelled into the city on the relevant dates. In a lengthy interview at Luton police headquarters at the end of February detectives confronted him with their findings and Manton finally confessed.

From that point on he never denied killing his wife but always added the rider that it had been accidental. In the statement he eventually made to police he maintained that had she never thrown the tea over him she would have still been alive. That single action had been the cause of her death. It had been sudden, unexpected and had caused him to become momentarily disorientated. The stool, which he readily admitted had been the murder weapon, had only been intended to fend her off, a sort of shield to stop her attacking him. The blows he had delivered with it simply a reflex action, no more. He went on to explain that putting her body into the river was the only way he could think of to keep the death of their mother from his children.

It certainly had the ring of truth about it but there could be no denying, given the extent of Irene's injuries, that Manton had committed murder. When he finally appeared in court toward the end of May 1944 he must have known that his chances of acquittal were nil and a manslaughter verdict little better; particularly after pathologist, Keith Simpson, had taken the stand to tell the court of his post-mortem findings. Irene had sustained severe injuries to her jaw and ear on the left side of her face:

> *The ear had been split and all the bones of the head loosened by a blow or blows. The lower jaw was fractured and there were one or more fractures through the neck of the jaw bone. In addition there was a gaping wound on the back of the head. Injuries to the neck showed Mrs Manton had been gripped in front and had struggled to free herself . . .*

He went on to explain that in his opinion at some point she had been pinned on her back, either to a wall or the floor, where an attempt to strangle her had been made. But the signs were she had escaped before being struck violently across the left side of her face. That had been followed by a second blow, which had knocked her to the ground and she had then been tied up by string whilst still alive, though unconscious.

Damning stuff and followed by testimony from Irene's sister who claimed to have witnessed Manton striking his wife on an earlier occasion, something he had vehemently denied when originally questioned by police. But the very fact that it had been raised in open court negated his plea of innocence. Manton's whole defence depended upon him being able to show that the fight with Irene had been a one off, a totally isolated incident. Only then would his defence counsel have legitimate grounds for pleading manslaughter. So, as the prosecution case closed, Bertie Manton was brought to the stand to explain in his own words the state of his marriage, his attitude toward his dead wife and just exactly what had happened on that November afternoon in 1943.

Under skilful questioning from his defence counsel, Arthur Ward, he told of how he and Irene had met, the birth of his children, his work, his relationship with his mother-in-law and how things had begun to go badly wrong after his wife had changed her job. At some length he told the court how, in his opinion, her new found friends had proven a detrimental influence upon his marriage. The job, he told the jury, had a social life attached that neither had expected, but that Irene for some reason had embraced wholeheartedly, over the space of twelve months changing her from doting mother to carousing party-goer. Sobriety abandoned in pursuit of some form of social acceptance. This, he claimed, had been the key factor in creating the animosity that slowly developed between the two of them. He could no longer rely upon her, she stayed out late, drank too much and even seemed to resent his presence in her life, which inevitably led to arguments. Though he vehemently denied these were ever violent, even the fight in November resulting in her death, he insisted, could have been avoided, murder he claimed, had never been his intention, it had all been a dreadful accident.

In his summing up to the jury, Mr Justice Singleton was sceptical of Manton's claims of provocation and that the killing of his wife had been unintentional:

> . . . *You may think that the first thing a husband or a decent man, as this man is said to be, having brought about an injury to his wife, whether fatal or otherwise, would do would be to send for some help . . . I think it is fair to imagine that in the three months that had passed since his wife's death he had spent some time in thinking what he should say if the body proved to be his wife's. There were only two people present when Mrs Manton received the injuries. You have had an account from the accused. You cannot have any account from the other. She is dead. It may well be a fact for you to bear in mind when you are filled with pity for a man on his trial that not much has been said about the one who is dead . . . We don't know what the woman would have said had she been alive. You may wonder whether she was as black as he has said . . .*

It took the jury an agonising two and a quarter hours to arrive at a decision. When it came it was that Manton was guilty of murder. He was duly sentenced to death.

A petition for reprieve was quickly raised on the grounds that much of the judge's summing up had been both biased and erroneous. When the appeal was heard in June, before Lord Caldecote, the Lord Chief Justice, defence counsel from the original trial, Arthur Ward, cited six key points in law that he claimed had prejudiced Manton's right to justice; though in essence only two were significant. They were that the judge had failed to give direction to the jury with regard to manslaughter, and that he had also not accepted that Manton's statement regarding the killing provided sufficient ground for provocation to have been a key factor.

After due consideration the appeal was rejected. Lord Caldecote was not convinced by the defence team's argument and Manton's execution date was set for 5 July. Immediately the news arrived in Luton a second petition was raised and submitted to the Home Secretary along with 29,659 signatories. This time it worked and twenty-four hours before he was due to die, the sentence was commuted to one of life.

CHAPTER 15

A Moment of Madness

The Death of Phyllis Shields
Stotfield, 1960

Exactly why Hilde had fired the fatal shots was a mystery.

When Chief Inspector Oliver walked into the lounge of Brookend, a house on Castle's Close, Stotfold, at ten minutes to eleven on the night of 2 September 1960, he discovered an automatic pistol carefully placed on the coffee table, one spent cartridge case beside it and a body on the floor. The body was that of forty-three-year-old Phyllis Shields. She had been shot once in the left side of her chest, the bullet penetrating her heart, and once in the back. Death had been near instantaneous. In one of the bedrooms upstairs he found Hilde Maria Adams, German by birth, sat on the bed. She was calm and, as the policeman entered the room, she told him she had murdered the woman in the lounge below.

Exactly why Hilde had fired the fatal shots was a mystery. Possibly jealous, Hilde had been living away from her husband, a scrap dealer, since April and had only returned to what she described as her home that night. When she had entered the house she had shot Phyllis dead and waited for the police. They took her to Biggleswade police station where she was formally charged with murder. She made no attempt to deny the charge and signed a statement acknowledging her guilt. Seven days later she appeared at Biggleswade magistrates' court accompanied by a policeman, a prison officer and a nurse. Pathologist, Dr J Williams, told the court that the dead woman would never have survived the two shots, which were fired from close range, and death had resulted from haemorrhage caused by the wound to the heart. No other evidence was heard and Hilde was remanded into custody.

It was the end of January 1961 before the public saw her a second time when her trial opened at Bedford Assize Court. But in the intervening months Hilde had been held in secure

Castles Close, Stotfold. The author

custody in Holloway and subjected to rigourous medical examinations. Dr Mervyn Williams, Holloway's senior medical officer told the presiding judge, Mr Justice Havers, that Hilde had said nothing about the killing, though she had never denied carrying it out. The motive remained unclear, but what he had discovered was that Hilde had suffered various mental troubles or disorders going back to 1954. He also told the court that on four separate occasions it appeared she had been diagnosed as suffering from schizophrenia and hospitalised. Two of those occasions had been voluntary admissions, both after having been certified. Throughout her incarceration, he added, the symptoms of schizophrenia were again clearly evident:

> *At present she is suffering paranoiac schizophrenia, which is the disease, which has previously been diagnosed when she has been in hospital. She is showing very gross signs indeed of that now.*

From the witness box Hilde Adames strongly disagreed and constantly interrupted the doctor's testimony, shouting, 'Yes, I am fit to plead, I cannot sleep if I cannot plead.' At that point

Stotfold cemetery where Phyllis Shield was buried. The author

Mr Justice Havers stopped proceedings and asked the jury, in light of the Holloway doctor's evidence, to retire and decide whether or not they felt Hilde was fit to plead on the grounds of her being insane. Within minutes they had agreed with the medical opinion and the trial was brought to an abrupt end. Hilde was sentenced to be detained in a mental hospital, where she would stay for life.

So the circumstances surrounding the appalling death of Phyllis Shields were never aired in open court. There seems little doubt that Hilde Adams suffered from serious mental illness and obviously for that reason alone it would have been impossible to proceed. Unfortunate, though, for Phyllis's family who had travelled up from London, Phyllis's home, and were never to receive closure on her death.

CHAPTER 16

Tragedy on Deadman's Hill

The Hanratty Case
Bedford, 1961

Be quiet, I am finking.

On 22 August 1961 twenty-five-year-old Valerie Storie left the Road Research Laboratory, Slough, where she worked as laboratory assistant, at around 5.30 pm. Outside, she met scientist, Michael Gregston. The two had known each other since the summer of 1958, they worked together and despite Gregston being a married man were having an affair. That night they had decided to have a quiet drink together in the *Old Station Inn,* a pub in Taplow, on the outskirts of Slough. Mad keen on car rallying – they had done some twenty or so together – he the driver she the navigator, and they wanted to plan the next event. When they had finished their drinks they went for a drive to Dorney Reach, not far from Windsor. There they pulled the car, a grey, Morris Minor 1000, off the road and into a cornfield. The time was a little after a quarter to nine.

Some three quarters of an hour later, just as it began to get dark, a man approached the car and tapped on the driver's window. Curious, Gregston wound it down to halfway at which point a gun was thrust into his face and a voice told him to open the door.

This is a hold up. I am a desperate man. I have been on the run four months. You do as I tell you and you will be all right.

Gregston did as he was instructed but the gunman had no intention of driving. Instead, he pulled open the back door and climbed in behind them. Pointing the gun at their heads, he ordered the couple to hand over their watches and any money. Gregston gave him £3, Valerie managed to hide hers in her bra, the two watches he gave back. Then, as if to reinforce the view that he was serious, he rattled the ammunition in his pockets, but he made no attempt to leave. Over the next hour he told them he was on the run, that every police force across Britain were after him, and that he had been sleeping rough for the last two days. Waving the gun about to indicate its likeness to those seen in Hollywood films, he told the couple he felt like a cowboy. For a brief moment he was animated, excited, and his actions were childlike, but there was no doubting the weapon, which was later identified as a .38 Enfield revolver, was very real and equally deadly.

At half-past ten, an hour after the anonymous gunman had clambered into the Morris Minor's rear seat, a light went on in a nearby house. As if shocked by the sudden realisation that people lived in such close proximity, the gunman was immediately unnerved. In a moment of brief panic he sat bolt upright, waved the revolver at them and, in a voice laced with threat, told them they would be shot if it brought out any inquisitive neighbours. All eyes turned toward the house. Then the light clicked off again and the crisis passed. If they had needed any convincing that the man sat behind them was dangerous that was the vital moment. For the next half hour or so they all sat quietly in the dark.

At around 11 pm their captor told them he wanted to eat. Gesturing toward Gregston he told him to get out of the car and into the boot, it was time for a change of driver. Gregston began to open the door but in a sudden show of defiance Valerie stopped him. The exhaust was cracked; she knew if he were shut inside the boot the fumes would kill him. It would be better, she told the gunman having explained all that, if he were left behind the wheel. Besides, he knew the car better than a stranger. The argument was persuasive enough and the gunman finally agreed, telling them to drive to Slough.

At a quarter to midnight they were on Slough High Street, but they made no stop. Instead, some half an hour later they pulled into Kingsbury Circle garage, Wembley, where they bought petrol, and at about 1 am stopped again this time at Stanmore, north of Harrow, to buy cigarettes from a machine for Gregston, a place the gunman seemed familiar with. To the two in front of the car it was just an aimless meandering drive across north London, and they hoped at any stage of it the gunman would stop the car and leave. But he appeared to have no intentions of ever releasing them. Instead, all he did was talk. None-stop dialogue about himself, his past, his association with the police and his criminal activities – which he claimed were many, though he was always careful not too give too much of himself away; except perhaps for his strong Cockney accent, that he made no attempt to disguise.

At around a half-past one in the morning he told Gregston to head north. He then turned the car toward St Albans, flicking his reversing lights on and off throughout the journey in a vain attempt to attract other motorist's attention. If the police been following the idea would have had serious merit, as it was it made no impact so he stopped. At Luton they turned on to the A6 for Bedford and at the Deadman's Hill lay-by, Clophill, the gunman, told them to stop and turn off all the lights. There, he told them he needed to sleep and, gesturing to Gregston with the gun, told him to get out of the car. The two men then went to the boot and returned with a length of rope from the car's toolbox. Climbing back into the rear of the Morris Minor, he told Valerie to lean forward and, reaching into the front seat, he tied her hands behind her back. At that point he noticed a duffle bag at Valerie's feet. With no rope left to tie up Gregston he suddenly realised the bag's rope fastenings would work just as efficiently, and so asked for the bag to be passed back to him. Gregston reached down, lifted it into the air and was in the

Deadman's Hill today. The author

process of passing it over the back of Valeries' seat when the gunman fired twice. Both bullets hit Gregson in the head and killed him outright. As he slumped back into his seat she screamed out at him:

You shot him. You bastard, why did you do that?

The only answer he could give was that the sudden movement had frightened him. Valerie, her voice understandably raised through a combination of shock and fear, shouted at him to fetch a doctor or at least let her take the car to go find one. But the gunman, probably panicked by her reaction and uncertain himself about what to do, pushed the revolver at her and told her to be quiet.

Be quiet, I am finking.

It was a phrase that would eventually hang him and as he uttered it his face was momentarily caught in the headlights of a passing car. For the first time that night Valerie Storie saw the pale face, brown hair and piercing eyes of her abductor. He saw her clearly too and both must have known what was likely to happen next. The gunman ordered her out of the car and told her she must remove Gregston's body from the driving seat and carry it into the lay-by. She initially refused but he insisted. He told her he could not be any where near the body in case he got blood on his suit. It was at that point she realised just how well-dressed her abductor actually was, particularly for a man supposed to have been sleeping rough. But he still had the gun and so she did as she was told to do. Once he was happy with where the body had been placed he ordered her into the back of the car, untied her hands and raped her.

Immediately after the attack he ordered her back out onto the road and told her to lie face down. As she did so she gave him a £1 note, told him it was all she had and asked him to leave her and go. He took her money then began to walk away and, for a moment, it appeared she would be safe. But then he turned back and fired five shots into her back; reloading he fired another two, which missed, then walked over to where she lay and kicked her to be sure she was dead. Valerie made not a sound. Satisfied, he then climbed into the Morris and drove away. The time was about 3 am.

Valerie Storie had been paralysed from the waist down but was still very much alive. For the next three-and-a-half hours,

Clophill village today. The author

in between bouts of unconsciousness, she tried hard to attract passing traffic with little success. In fact it was not until 6 30 am that she and Michael Gregston were first seen. Haynes labourer Sydney Burton, on his way to work, saw what he thought had been some sort of road accident. Without stopping to help, he ran over to the RAC box, which stood further along Deadman's Hill. There, he found student John Kerr just setting up for his day to monitor traffic movements for a government traffic census. Kerr was then first on the scene. Valerie by this time had lost an awful lot of blood but was still conscious. There was nothing he could do, her injuries were so severe and outside his limited first aid capabilities. After flagging down several cars he sent their drivers off in search of police and an ambulance, then settled down to wait.

Detective Superintendent Charles Barron, Bedfordshire's CID chief, followed the medical team, and immediately instructed that Gregston's body was to remain where he lay until the crime scene could be secured. A ten-foot high canvas screen was placed around the murder scene, and two army sappers were called in to sweep the area with mine detectors. They found nothing. Meanwhile, acting on information from Valerie Storie, police officers were sent to Michael Gregston's home, tasked with informing his wife, Janet, of his death. She made a formal identification just after three o'clock in the afternoon.

Meanwhile, Valerie Storie was taken to Bedford General Hospital from where she furnished police with a reasonably good description of her attacker. *Bedfordshire Times* published that description in their evening editions and it quickly went national:

> *Wanted. A man described as being about 30 years of age, 5ft 6ins in height, medium build, pale-ish face, dark hair, clean-shaven, brown eyes, wearing a dark lounge suit.*

Later that same day, Scotland Yard were called in and Detective Superintendent Robert Acott took charge of the case.

From the outset, he believed the killer to be from the capital. Everything Valerie Storie had managed to tell him about the man, what he had said in the car, his apparent familiarity with some of the places they had passed through, the fact he had

Maulden village today. The author

DEADMAN'S HILL MURDER HUNT

THE hunt for the A.6 gunman goes on as hundreds of reports continue to pour into the murder headquarters at Bedford from people who claim to have seen the person in the Identi-kit pictures issued by the police earlier this week.

Miss Valerie Storie (25), of Cippenham, Bucks., who was seriously injured in the shooting at Deadman's Hill, Clophill, was moved from Bedford General Hospital (South Wing) yesterday (Thursday) to Guys Hospital, London.

Here she will undergo an operation for the removal of two of the bullets which are lodged deeply inside her.

Dr. Keith Simpson, the pathologist and firearms expert, who examined her in Bedford General Hospital last Saturday to learn more about the exact manner in which she sustained her gunshot injuries, will be present at the operation.

Miss Storie has gone to Guys because it is at this hospital that Dr. Simpson is a Reader in Forensic Medicine.

Yesterday, Det.-Supt. Charles Barron, head of Bedfordshire CID, gave an up-to-the-minute description of the gunman compiled from reports of several witnesses.

His most striking feature is his icy blue large, saucer-like eyes. He is aged between 25 and 30, about 5 ft. 6 in. tall and proportionate in build, has dark brown hair, and is clean shaven.

It is known the killer was wearing a dark lounge suit and collar and tie on the night of the murder, so police are concentrating their search for a man of neat and clean appearance.

Since the Identi-kit pictures were issued to the Press and television on Tuesday, reports from places as far apart as

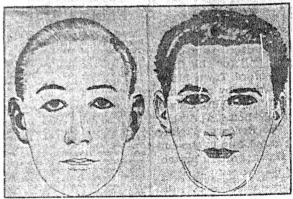

These are the Identi-kit pictures built up from the impressions of witnesses, and are those of a man the police wish to interview in connexion with the crime. Any information as to the identity of the man should be given to the Chief Constable, Bedfordshire Constabulary, County Police H.Q., Bedford, or to any police station.

Scotland, Wales, and the south and east coasts have come in to the murder hunt detectives, who have set up their headquarters in the lecture room

---

At 10 p.m. on Monday Miss Mavis Valentine, of High Street, Houghton Conquest, was found lying on the grass verge directly opposite the murder spot. She had been taken ill. A police dog was used to search the area, but nothing was found to associate the incident with the shooting.

---

at the County Police Headquarters at The Pines, Goldington Road, Bedford.

Most of the messages are from people who say they have

seen the person shown in the Identi-kit pictures and every report is being closely followed up.

So far, as a result of these messages, about 12 people have been taken into police stations for questioning about their movements on the night of the murder, but they were all released when police were satisfied that they were not connected with it.

On the night of Tuesday-Wednesday, just one week after the shooting in which Mr. Michael Gregsten (34), of Abbots Langley, was killed, teams of detectives stopped vehicles on roads between Slough and Deadman's Hill. Drivers were shown the Identi-kit pictures and asked if they could help.

Some of the police officers who are engaged on the Clophill murder case are seen at work in the operations room at The Pines.

The two identi-kit pictures of the murder suspect. The *Bedford Times* originally been on foot and, of course, the man's Cockney accent, all supported his view that they were searching for a Londoner. If he were a fugitive then Acott believed it was also highly likely that he had no fixed address but would be likely to stay where he could move on quickly. He therefore ordered that an appeal go out to all hotels and guest-houses to report any strange or suspicious guests. National newspapers ran the story over the following few days.

The Morris Minor was found in Ilford two days later, though with no serious clues as to its last driver. That led to two witnesses coming forward to say they had seen the car on the morning of the murder. James Trower claimed to have seen the car being parked by the killer; and John Skillett claimed to have argued with the driver. From a police point of view Skillett's was the better eyewitness account. He stated that the driver had deliberately hampered him on the road at around 7 am on 23 August. Incensed by the lack of courtesy, he had pulled in behind the Morris when it stopped and argued with its driver. That led to Skillett and Valerie Storie to each produce an identi-kit picture of the man they had seen, which was then published in all national and local newspapers.

But the first real breakthrough came on 24 August when Edwin Cooke lifted the back seat of a number 36A London bus. For him it was a matter of routine, something he did every day as part of his job working as a cleaner for London Transport. He knew that it was the only seat on the bus that could be easily lifted, and had often been used as a dump for rubbish – and the occasionally dead rat, by some of their less than salubrious passengers. What he found there this time though was far from mundane. Staring back at him from the dark recess was a .38 Enfield revolver and ammunition wrapped inside a handker-chief. Later police tests revealed that he had found the A6 murder weapon.

This and the car confirmed Acott's hunch that the killer had not stayed in Bedford but had gone to ground somewhere in London. Next came a call from a hotel in response to the detec-tive's earlier appeal. According to the manager, one particular guest had refused to leave his room for several days, which he considered to be suspicious. Police agreed and the man in question, Frederick Durant, was brought in for questioning. But after checks were made as to his movements he was given an alibi by his mother for the night of the murder and found to have stayed at a seedy hotel, the *Vienna*, Maida Vale, on the following night, so he was released.

For the next few days, little happened and the investigation was in danger of stalling. Then came an astonishing discovery. Juliana Galvez, a Spanish cleaner at the *Vienna Hotel*, the place Frederick Durant had stayed, found two spent cartridge shells in room 24. Subsequent forensic examination showed that they had been fired from the same revolver found on the London bus. Acott was convinced that the killer had stayed at that hotel either the night before the murder or during the week before, and had fired the gun to test its capability. Then, probably through simple carelessness, had left the spent shells behind. All they needed was to find the man that had stayed in that room and they had their killer.

William Nudds, manager of the *Vienna* was immediately brought into police headquarters for questioning. He initially told Acott that a man named Jim or James Ryan had stayed in room 24. He later changed that statement and said Ryan had stayed in room 6 and it had been Durant in the room where the cartridges were found. He also told police that Durant was an alias for a man named Peter Alphon. Acott then took the unusual step of publicly naming Alphon as a murder suspect and letting the press run an appeal for information. That brought him to the surface and on 22 September he surrendered himself to Scotland Yard. Two days later he was placed into an identity parade held at Guys Hospital where Valerie Storie had been taken from Bedford. But she failed to pick him out, instead identifying a stranger used to make up the suspect line, and Alphon was later released.

Acott then raided the *Vienna Hotel* and pulled its manager in a second time. If Alphon had not been the guest in room 24, manager Nudds had to have known who was. But Nudds himself had a reputation for dishonesty when it came to his dealings with the law, as Acott well knew. In 1958 he had been released from prison after serving nine years for car theft and obtaining money by deception. In all, he had a criminal record stretching back years and had been known to use any one of fourteen different aliases. So, when they met a second time the interview took on a slightly different dimension. This time the Scotland Yard man was not going to be brushed aside so easily. This time he demanded Nudds tell the truth and this time he did. In fact, he began his statement with an apology and then admitted that when he had told Acott about Alphon being in room 24 it had only been because he wanted to help. Bizarrely, it seemed that Nudds had been of the opinion that the police case against Alphon had been so strong it only needed his support for a conviction. So he had given it in the hope they would then go away and leave him alone. Conscience, he told Acott, caused him to admit he had lied. The real occupant of room 24 had been Jim Ryan and the Ryan was an alias for James Hanratty.

Hanratty was twenty-five years old, and well known to police. He had one key distinguishing feature, his hair. It was ginger, which made him easy to spot if seen, so over the years he had taken to dying it either brown or black – something he had done ever since his initial brush with the law back in 1954 when he was arrested for stealing a car. It was a crime for which he received twelve months probation and, in that same year, he was sentenced to four years for housebreaking. Two-and-a-half years later he was back on the street and arrested in Brighton for car theft. That put him back in prison for nine months and this was followed by a further stint in prison in 1958 when he served three years in Strangeways. Since his release he had been known to have been active in and around London where he had burgled a number of houses and stolen a significant amount of jewellery – but had not, so far, been caught.

Acott was certain that this time they had a tangible lead and, as he had done with Alphon, he had his name released to the press. But finding Hanratty was never going to be easy. An accomplished car thief and housebreaker, he rarely stayed in one place long enough to be caught, tending instead to move between various houses, hotels and his parents. Most were scattered across London but he had been known to travel to Luton, Bedford, Manchester and occasionally to Ireland. In all these places he had contacts, people who lived in his dark world so to speak, and people who could be useful to him. Most operated on the fringe of the law, some were ex-cons, others he knew from prison. But certainly all would have known his background and also that, since the late 1950s, jewellery had become his key money earner. It was easier to conceal, less conspicuous when moving it around and paid well. Add to that the occasional antique and it would probably be fair to say Hanratty considered he was doing well. Over the years experience had taught him which items were valuable and which were not. In turn that had made his burglary activities extremely lucrative, and any items he was unsure of were taken to St John's Wood. There he stayed with Charles France, 'Dixie' to his friends, who knew about jewellery and would help fill in the blanks. Charlotte, Dixie's wife, did his washing and ironing and daughter, Carol Ann, often dyed his hair. For Hanratty their house became one of two key locations he used regularly, and one he considered safe. The other was near Soho.

In July 1961, using his alias of Jim Ryan, he had met Louise Anderson, an attractive blond with an antique shop on Soho's Greek Street. To Hanratty's profligate eye she was a perfect business partner. He needed another outlet for his older pieces of jewellery and she needed to make money. Throughout the summer he nurtured the relationship and by early autumn she was an integral part of his corruption. In turn that gave him access to her London flat, which he used regularly, and where he often left suitcases to be collected at later dates.

So, for Scotland Yard, breaking into this fairly wide circle was not going to be easy. But when Hanratty saw his name blazoned across the national press it was he who made the first contact. On 5 October 1961, he rang Dixie France and told him what he had seen in the newspapers and asked what he should do. France was in no doubt that he had to contact police and advised him to make contact with Scotland Yard. It was better, he told Hanratty, if he put his case first before they could make any arrest. So, on the following day, he took France's advice and made three calls to Superintendent Acott's office. But Hanratty had chosen a bad day to make contact. Acott was in Bedford and not available. So Hanratty caught a train and travelled to Blackpool. From there, he made a fourth phone call, this time successfully and five days later he was arrested after leaving a café, by Detective Constable James Williams.

Detective superintendent Acott travelled to Blackpool overnight and on 12 October, Hanratty was interviewed for the first time. At that interview – as expected – he claimed never to have met either Michael Gregston or Valerie Storie, and denied any involvement in the A6 murder. In his initial statement he told Acott that he had in fact been in Liverpool for a number of days at the end of August, including the day of the shooting. The visit had been criminal in nature, in other words the men he met could ill afford a visit from the police. For that reason he told the detective he could not give names and addresses for fear of incriminating them in some way in other crimes. Acott was far from convinced. He reminded Hanratty that they were questioning him about a murder, a particularly vile, and horrific murder and one that carried a capital charge. If he had been in Liverpool he would need to prove it. But Hanratty was adamant and refused to give any other detail. At Bedford next day he was picked out from a line-up by John Skillet, the driver who claimed to have had an argument with him hours after the killing.

Twenty-four hours later he was driven down to Stoke Mandeville hospital, which was where Valerie Storie had been taken to aid her recovery, and placed in a second identity line up with thirteen other men. Each man had been given a number, Hanratty was number six. Valerie was then wheeled into the room but before passing along the line asked the super-intendent if it would be possible for each man to say – *Be quiet will you, I'm thinking*. He agreed. She was then slowly wheeled along the line three times, each man speaking in turn. At that point she turned to the inspector and indicated the number 6. Hanratty, apart from being a close match to Valerie's original description had also been the only man unable to pronounce the diphthong 'TH', instead he used 'F' causing him to pronounce thinking as 'finking'. Later that day he was formally charged with murder.

He made his first appearance in public at Bedford's Ampthill magistrates' court, on 16 October. Outside, reporters and photographers lined Church Street, the narrow approach to the courthouse, their numbers swelled by a huge crowd of onlookers all eager to catch a glimpse of the A6 murderer. Though most were disappointed, Hanratty hid himself beneath a raincoat for the dash from car to court. Inside, he pleaded not guilty, Acott explained how he had been arrested and charged, and he was then remanded back to prison. The hearing lasted no more than six minutes. Seven days later he was back. The second hearing, whilst still brief, was distinctly acrimonious. Hanratty's defence team were angered by the Crown's refusal to divulge evidence and exchange information. Barrister Michael Sherrard, told the court that had it not been for the press he would not have been aware of the discovery of the murder weapon:

> *We are somewhat hampered from our point of view, in making our own enquiries, because we do not know at what time and indeed on what precise day it is alleged that the murder took place . . . Arising out of that and giving rise to the same considerations, we understand – and we only know this from the press – that on some day after the murder and the attack on Miss Storie, a gun was found on an omnibus. We should like to know the date and the time when that gun was found, if possible . . .*

There followed a lengthy debate between the defence, the magistrates and the police, represented on this occasion by a Superintendent Morgan, but with no success gained by the

The main entrance into the Shire Hall court.
The author

Hanratty team, police insisting that timescales were such that they had not completed their own investigations, and would not divulge any further information until that process had been completed. Hanratty was remanded a second time. This continued throughout November until a trial date for the end of January was finally fixed.

Hanratty took his place in the dock of Bedford's Shire Hall court before Mr Justice Gorman, on the afternoon of Monday 22 January 1962. Again, he pleaded not guilty. By this time so much had been written about the A6 murder to heighten public interest that, unlike at the earlier hearings, crowds were far more difficult to control. Their numbers had been building all morning, fuelled by the daily news reports, which suggested this was to be the show trial of the twentieth century so far – people wanted to be a part of the drama as it unfolded. So, for the duration of the trial, they filled the pavements round about, satisfied just to watch the comings and goings of those who were to be the central characters. The stage was set for what would be one of the longest and most contentious murder trials in British legal history.

In his opening address to the court, prosecuting counsel, Mr Graham Swanwick, was circumspect in his handling of the detail surrounding the trial. Carefully listing the salient points upon which the Crown had built its case, and explaining how they would be proven as the trial progressed. He then explained to the jury how Michael Gregston and Valerie Storie had essentially been kidnapped at gunpoint, of the long car journey they had endured, the circumstances of Gregston's eventual murder, and the comprehensive police investigation that followed. Then, turning toward Hanratty, he told how his identity had been uncovered, how he had been linked to the killing, and how whilst in Brixton prison on remand he had confessed his guilt to fellow inmate, Roy Langdale. As he resumed his seat after what had been an extremely lengthy speech a buzz of excitement rippled around the public gallery. No one had heard before any mention of a confession, though for defence counsel, Michael Sherrard, who had obviously been informed of Langdale's allegation, it made little difference. He knew there was far more cogent evidence to be heard before the deposition of a discredited Finchley greengrocer would be put to the court. All of which he would have to challenge and most of which he believed to be far more damaging to James Hanratty than that of an ex-con. That began with the testimony of Valerie Storie.

Accompanied by a nurse and physiotherapist, she was brought into court later that afternoon. The *Bedfordshire Times* reported that she appeared calm. No doubt that was not the case. Nevertheless, she told the jury, in some detail, of what had happened to her and Michael Gregston back in August of the previous year. Using a map as an aid, she outlined the journey the three of them had made. The various stops were explained, why they had been made, and how, in an effort to keep the gunman calm, she had kept him talking throughout most of the car journey. Reiterating the point about the man's inability to pronounce words beginning with 'Th' and always substituting the letter 'f', she told the jury his accent was therefore not only distinct but also recognisable. Then in a raised voice she began to detail the events surrounding the death of Michael Gregston;

how all had been well up until he reached for the duffle bag and how the gunman, without any provocation at all, shot him twice as he tried to pass the bag into the back of the car. At that point, she told the court, she had begun screaming hysterically and then, as she calmed down, tried to snatch the gun away from his grip, but he had been too strong. In the almost eerie silence of the courtroom she then told how she was forced to remove Gregston's body from the car; how she struggled to drag the dead man into the lay-by out of sight of the main road, and of how the gunman then raped her on the car's back seat before shooting her five times in the back. At that point prosecutor, Graham Swanwick rose to his feet and asked the pertinent question: Was the man responsible for carrying out those acts James Hanratty? In a loud voice charged with emotion she turned to stare across the twenty feet that separated her from where he sat in the dock, saying:

I have no doubt at all that this was the man who shot Mike and myself.

Valerie's unequivocal condemnation of Hanratty was never going to be overcome, and for the defence it simply got worse.

From the outset of the case Hanratty had never changed his story. From the moment of his arrest he had insisted that on the dates in question he had been in Liverpool, where he had stayed for several days. In fact so insistent had he been about that fact that despite the lack of corroborating evidence, which appeared to have made no impact upon him, his defence team had been forced to accept it as a legitimate alibi. It was of course a lie and a lie that was to cost Hanratty dear.

The defence strategy therefore, was simple enough: prove the prosecution had no case. In order to do that they needed to first cast a seed of doubt over Valerie Storie's evidence. She was the only eyewitness and her testimony was pivotal. In order that they could do that they had to be able to show that her evidence was flawed. This they attempted to do in two ways. Firstly, the identification evidence, her original description published by the press hours after the attack differed significantly to that used to identify Hanratty. He, for example, had blue eyes not brown and was shorter in height. Secondly, that on the first identification parade, attended by Peter Alphon who at that time had been the police's number one suspect, she picked out an innocent member of the public. Both were valid arguments and no doubt did cast some doubt.

The entrance to the rear of Shire Hall where thousands gathered on each day of the trial. The author

But that alone was simply not enough. With Hanratty remaining stubborn over his Liverpool visit all that remained was to mount an attack on the *Vienna Hotel* evidence. Room 24 was the next piece of crucial evidence and the identity of its occupant on 21 August vital. Forensics had already proven beyond doubt that the cartridges found on the bedroom floor matched the murder weapon. It was a proven fact that only two single men had checked into the hotel that week and both on the 21st. Those men were Peter Alphon and James Hanratty, although both men used aliases. One of them was a murderer, but which one? The defence believed it was Peter Alphon. He fit the original description, he had a police record, was a sexual predator, and had already been shown to have stayed the night in the *Vienna Hotel*. Manager, William Nudds, they argued, was an unreliable witness. He had already lied once about room 24 and, they believed, he had absolutely no idea which of the two men had stayed in that room on the crucial night. But when Nudds took the stand, despite being blitzed by questions from the defence counsel, he was immovable. So was Charlotte France, Dixie's wife. She told the court that Hanratty had shown her a billhead with the *Vienna Hotel* emblazoned across the top and the date stamp of 21 August. Damning maybe, but that still did not prove he had spent the night in the crucial hotel room, though it certainly shattered the notion that he could have been in Liverpool on that night, although it did not preclude him travelling north on the following day.

When Peter Alphon was not then called by the prosecution as a witness it negated any further chance the defence team had of challenging the validity of William Nudd's statement. But it also did more than that. It meant that doubts over the occupant of room 24 would remain unresolved, and the burden of evidence would continue to support the prosecution assertion that it had been Hanratty.

At the end of the first two days it is fair to say the prosecution were on track to prove their case and it continued that way for much of the trial. Evidence was heard from Dixie France to the effect that he had been told by Hanratty that he used the upstairs back seats of buses, because they could be lifted out of place, to disguard stolen items that were of no value. The two motorists, John Skillett and James Trower, reprised their early statements about having seen Hanratty at the wheel of the

Bedford Prison as Hanratty would have seen it. Author's collection

Morris Minor hours after the killing. Louise Anderson admitted her guilt over handling stolen goods and selling them on through her antique shop, whilst various women confirmed they had dyed his ginger hair on various occasions – to aid his disguise. Then, the defence brought into court Roy Langdale.

At the time of the trial Roy Langdale, one time London grocer, was serving three years probation for carrying out Post Office savings forgeries, and had just been released from Brixton Prison, a place he was familiar with having been convicted previously of assault, theft and stealing a car. Whilst Hanratty had been held on remand in the same prison he claimed the two of them had met on a daily basis during exercise. In his testimony he told the court that Hanratty had talked to him about the case, had confessed to being the A6 murderer, and expressed dismay at Valerie Storie's survival:

He said he shot Gregston, took Valerie in the back and raped her. He told me he didn't take Gregston from the car, but Valerie did. He told her to lay down and then he shot her in cold blood, and then he laughed about it . . . He said he took the car; all he was interested in was the girl. He said about Valerie's condition that he was sorry that she was still living because she could identify him and without her there could be no identification . . . The main subject he talked about was girls and sex and fings like that . . .

But Langdale was an opportunist and under fierce cross-examination by Hanratty's counsel, who was desperate to discredit his evidence, he was forced to admit that he had already accepted £25 from the *Sunday Pictorial* to sell his story; and the *Daily Herald* had also offered him £20, which he had turned down. In fact, as Sherrard pointed out, a photograph of Langdale had appeared in the *Pictorial* before the trial had even begun, something he confessed he had engineered himself by calling the newspaper the minute he realised he was to become a prosecution witness. At which point Sherrard accused him of being nothing but a liar, a man without scruples who would do absolutely anything for money. Obviously Langdale refuted that but the damage had been done and his evidence seriously compromised, as the defence barrister had intended.

There then followed various witnesses who told the story of Hanratty's past, his criminal record, the discovery of the gun on the 36A bus, and of the enquiries made to prove his Liverpool alibi. The trial by this time had lasted ten days and the Crown's case was coming to a close. The last key witness for them was to be Detective Superintendent Acott. For two days he stood in the witness box and endured thirteen hours of questioning, so crucial was he to both sides of the courtroom.

For Acott there can be no doubt it was an ordeal, but clearly his evidence was vital to the success or failure of the defence case. After explaining to the jury just why Hanratty had become a suspect, the circumstances surrounding his eventual capture in Blackpool, and the statements he had made whilst in police custody, he mentioned for the first time that Hanratty had talked to him about owning a gun. This was something of a revelation, all the court had heard up until that point, was that he had no experience of firearms. Acott went on to explain that during questioning Hanratty had mentioned a 'fence' (someone who bought stolen goods) in Ealing, a man he had used on occasion to move items from various burglaries. According to the detective, Hanratty told him, whilst under caution, that he had told the man he wanted to stop the housebreaking to move into armed robbery, and asked if he could find him a gun. The superintendent had no corroborating evidence to support the statement but its effect on the court was obviously dramatic. Nothing else he spoke of caused a similar stir and as the prosecuting counsel resumed his seat all eyes focused upon Graham Sherrard.

When he rose to his feet in the hushed court the expectation was almost palpable. He was not about to disappoint. Vehemently, he launched into an attack of the detective's character, accusing him of being selective in the evidence he had brought to court. If there had been any doubt the questioning would be hostile that opening removed it. It also angered Acott who resented the accusation:

That is a disgraceful allegation to say that I have selected my evidence.

But Sherrard was undaunted and asked Superintendent Acott to explain more fully about how the conversation about the gun had come about. The detective explained that he had simply volunteered the information. Whilst talking about stolen goods in Ealing he told the barrister that he had made two crucial statements.

Hanratty: I said, I think I will pack up the jewellery lark and I asked him to get a shooter to do some stick-ups.

Acott: Are you trying to tell me that you got a gun from a man in Ealing?

Hanratty: He would not play and never got me one.

Acott explained to the court this was significant because Hanratty had always denied having anything to do with a gun. He told Sherrard that after he had said it he fell silent as if realising he had just incriminated himself. But as the defence counsel pointed out, just how significant was the statement when no proof existed to back it up. In other words Acott had no supporting evidence.

Sherrard then moved on to Valerie Storie's testimony at the start of the trial and her first identity line-up failure. In a series of questions about Peter Alphon he asked how he had become a suspect? Why he was ever questioned? Why the initial description of the killer had fit him more closely than it had Hanratty, and why Valerie Storie's description of her attacker had not been disregarded when it became clear Alphon was not the killer? Acott was adamant her description had always been right despite some discrepancies: `

I did depend on it from the day of the murder until today. I stand firm on her. She never altered one scrap, but despite my knowledge at this time of the difference in description of Alphon and the wanted man with the Glickberg statement (another name for William Nudds). I had no alternative but to get Alphon in and eliminate him and that is exactly what happened, sir . . . Of course I was confident Alphon was not picked out by any of the witnesses.

Whether he was confident has to be questionable. At that time Alphon was all they had as a suspect and had Valerie pointed him out at that first identification parade this would have been a very different trial, as Sherrard well knew. But Acott handled himself confidently in the witness box and despite the constant flow of questions he never moved away from his belief that Hanratty was guilty. Though he was forced to acknowledge that if, as Hanratty had constantly insisted, he had been in Liverpool on 22 August he could not have returned in time to be at Dorney Reach.

On day twelve, the prosecution finally closed its case and it was then left to the defence to show they had failed in their endeavour to bring the real killer of Michael Gregston to court.

They began by making a truly startling disclosure. During defence counsel Sherrard's opening speech to the jury he admitted that James Hanratty had lied about Liverpool. He told the court that it had been subterfuge, nothing more, nothing less, something the defendant had dreamed up simply because he never believed the police would accept his real alibi. On the day of the murder, counsel told the court that Hanratty had actually been in a boarding house in Rhyl:

> *Rhyl is now being combed by the defence for some trace of that boarding house, but whether people there will remember a casual visit in the August bank holiday season is very speculative.*

This really was an amazing turn around. The defence had effectively suddenly changed its whole case. After twelve long days during which both sides of the court had constantly referred to the Liverpool alibi, whether favourably or otherwise, Hanratty had effectively put his hands in the air and admitted he had lied. At that point, as the murmur that rippled around the public gallery fell away, James Hanratty left the dock and took his place in the witness box.

The *Bedford Times* described Hanratty as being, *neatly dressed in a navy blue suit with a white shirt, and cuffs showing prominently beyond his sleeves.* In a soft voice he told the court of his criminal past, and described in detail his recent activities around North London operating as a burglar. He also agreed that he had told Dixie France about the upstairs back seats of some buses being loose and easy to lift. He went on to confirm that he had from time to time used them as a place to discard jewellery he could not sell. Under guidance from the defence counsel, he told the court that he had intended to travel to Liverpool to sell some diamonds, the proceeds of a robbery but too big to sell in London at a good price; but on 21 August had stayed at the *Vienna Hotel*, though not in room 24. On 22 August, the following day, he had caught a train to Liverpool but from there, after failing to find a specific address where he thought the diamonds could be sold, he had boarded a coach and travelled on to Rhyl. There he booked himself into a boarding house. The seaside resort, he explained, was a place he was familiar with, having worked there on the fairground in 1961, and his intention had been to find a man named Terry Evans, someone he knew worked on the bumper cars at the fairground. On the day of the murder, after he failed to find Evans, he went to the cinema to watch *The Guns of Navarrone* and returned to London on 24 August. He then told the court about his movements after the murder and of why he had lied to Superintendent Acott:

> *When I first rang Mr Acott he was very interested to know my whereabouts on August 21st, 23rd, and 24th. I was a little bit confused myself, seeing my name in the papers and knowing that my mother, father, and brother were looking for me, because I knew myself that I had not done this horrible crime. So I tried in every way I could to help superintendent Acott, and when he asked me where I was on 22/23 August my reply was Liverpool.*

When asked why he had not admitted that he had been in Rhyl he said it was simply because he could not remember the name of the boarding house, or the street, or the name of the people that ran it. When Sherrard pressed him further about why he had persisted in the untruth he added that it was because he had been in prison:

> *I am a man with a prison record and I know that in such a trial of this degree it is vital for a man not to change his evidence . . .*

He then denied ever discussing the case with Roy Langdale, but accepted that he had mentioned a gun when interviewed by Superintendent Acott, though he insisted he had never been serious. Guns, he told the court, were not a part of what he did, he was a housebreaker not an armed robber. In later fierce exchanges with the prosecution toward the end of his testimony much of this was challenged, with the most provocative confrontation being reserved for the story about Rhyl. Here, the prosecution alleged he had lied and that the boarding house was a figment of his imagination:

> *The truth of this matter is that the boarding house does not exist and your visit to it on August 22-23 is just another lie.*

But they were possibly wrong and, as Hanratty finally left the witness box, the trial was about to take another twist.

Because he had been unable to name the guest house, or the street upon which it stood, he had been asked by the defence team to provide what ever detail he could that would help them find it. He told them the house had a green bathroom, a plant of some sort had stood in the hallway, and that he could hear trains shunting at night. On the sixteenth day of the trial, Mrs

Grace Jones, landlady of a guesthouse on Kinmel Street, Rhyl, stood in court and told the judge the house he had described was hers. She then pointed a finger in James Hanratty's direction and identified him as being the man that had been a guest on 22 August. For a moment it appeared the defence had made the breakthrough they so desperately needed. Had she been able to provide solid evidence to back up her testimony they knew the case would have been over, but there, unfortunately, Mrs Jones let herself down. The court wanted more than just her word, they wanted proof. To that end the prosecution ordered that any guest register be brought to Bedford for inspection.

The guesthouse possessed three of them and when finally produced in court on the last day of the trial, not one contained the name of Hanratty or his alias Ryan. Then, under rigorous cross-examination by the prosecution, she was forced to admit that though the registers were available for guests to sign that was not always the case. She also told the court some of the relevant dates had also been torn out and destroyed because her son had scribbled over the signatures. When prosecution barrister Graham Swanwick then produced three male guests who could all prove they had stayed on the key dates but could not identify Hanratty, she was totally discredited.

At eleven thirty on the morning of 15 February 1962 Michael Sherrard stood to make his closing speech to the jury. For the next six hours he spoke with passion and eloquence in an attempt to persuade them to acquit Hanratty, on the grounds that evidence did not exist to show beyond doubt that he had been in the car with Valerie Storie and Michael Gregston. The eyewitness evidence, he insisted, was flawed and was, as he had tried to show in the trial, a better fit for Peter Alphon. Why, he asked the jurors, was Alphon not brought to court? Why had the prosecution depended so much on the word of William Nudds? Both, he claimed, had reputations that should have rendered any evidence they either offered or had been party to, to have been tainted. Then, in a vitriolic attack on Superintendent Acott he was less than complimentary on the way he had handled the case:

Mr Acott's entire attitude reeks of stubborn pride and unshake-able confidence in his own judgement even when it is in error.

One by one he analysed the witness evidence as it had been presented, reprised all the key points and finally asked them to

Notice of appeal given by the defence

IT was announced on Monday night that James Hanratty is to be executed at Bedford Jail on Wednesday, March 7, at 8 a.m. This date has been fixed according to law, following the death sentence on Hanratty late on Saturday night after a jury at Bedford Assizes had found him Guilty of the A6 murder, but it is unlikely that the execution will in fact be carried out on that day.

Hanratty has given notice of appeal and it is likely to be three weeks before the appeal is heard in London. If his appeal fails a new date will be fixed.

In the meantime the fight for the life of Hanratty, who continues to protest his innocence, goes on and his solicitor, Mr. Emmanuel Kleinmann, has appealed for three people, who he thinks may help him, to come forward. They are a well dressed man who Hanratty says was with him in the train to Liverpool on August 22, and a young couple who, says Hanratty, kissed each other goodbye at Euston just before the train left. Hanratty, aged 25, of Kingsbury, North London, is lodged in the condemned cell at Bedford Jail.

Crowds at times 500 strong surged outside the Shire Hall, Bedford through the long, tense wait for the verdict on Saturday. The verdict came at 9.12 p.m.—9 hours 50 minutes after the jury had first retired—and at the end of the longest known murder trial in British Courts.

Tension in the Court room heightened as the crowds, filling every seat and overspilling into gangways waited anxiously for the jury's return as soon as it was known they were agreed. As the jury foreman said "Guilty" there was a loud anguished cry from a woman in the back seat of the public gallery, heard above the gasps from all over the Court room.

Mr. Stanley Carlton, the Deputy Clerk, immediately turned to Hanratty, now running his tongue nervously between his lips, and addressed him gravely. "Prisoner at the Bar you stand convicted of capital murder. Have you anything to say why sentence of the Court should not be passed upon you according to law?"

Hanratty, a short slim figure, his hair streaked where the red dye had grown out, answered clearly, "I am not innocent." Then realising the wrong choice of words he gulped and visibly fought for the right ones.

Seconds later he said, "I am innocent, my lord, and I will appeal. That is all I have to say at this stage."

In the already stilled Court room the Judge's Clerk, Mr. Eric Willoughby, recited the seemingly unnecessary but obligatory caution. "My lords, the Queen's Justices do strictly charge and command that all persons keep silence while sentence of death is passed upon the prisoner at the Bar upon pain of imprisonment."

He turned to red robed Mr. Justice Gorman and placed upon his head the black cloth cap.

The Judge, softly spoken, but whose every word could now be heard, looked directly at the prisoner, 20 feet from him, and said, "James Hanratty. The sentence of the Court is that you suffer death in the manner authorised by law and may God have mercy on your soul." Hanratty briskly turned and ran down the steps to his cell beneath the dock.

Beside the Judge, standing erect as sentence was passed, were the dignitaries who had sat with him on the Bench for the four long weeks of the trial: the High Sheriff (the Hon. Hugh Lawson Johnston), the Chaplain (the Rev. D. H. Leonard Williams), and the Deputy Under Sheriff (Mr. David Lines).

THANKS TO JURY

The jury—only 11 strong—who during their long deliberations had once returned to the Court room for further advice had come to the end of their onerous duties.

Discharging them from further attendance at the Assizes, the Judge told them, "I want to say that I have a very high value of the public service rendered by juries. I know of no higher public service and in discharging you I would like you to bear that in mind."

He then ordered that they would not be called for further jury service for ten years.

Hanratty had pleaded "Not guilty" to the capital murder by shooting of Michael John Gregsten, a 36-year-old physicist at the Deadman's Hill layby near Clophill, on August 23 last year. The prosecution also claimed that he shot and raped Gregsten's companion, Miss Valerie Storie.

RECORD RETIREMENT

The 68-year-old Judge ended his summing up—it lasted 10 hours 2 minutes—at 11.22 a.m. on Saturday.

He told the jury that arrangements had been made for their lunch to be taken to them and laid down that the only persons who should take the meal into their room should be the two constables who were sworn as jury bailiffs.

Police officers then left the Court loaded with boxes of exhibits which they carried upstairs to the large committee room overlooking the River Great Ouse.

Shortly afterwards the jury were led to this room and began to set yet another record—the longest retirement in a murder trial.

One of the jurors asked if they could have the daily transcripts of evidence but the Judge said they could not and explained "I have gone through the evidence with you."

The same juror then asked for a list of witnesses and two copies were handed to the jury.

Because of the exceptional number of exhibits, 136 in all, the retiring room usually used by juries was considered inadequate.

A pot of tea was taken to the Judge's room about 10 minutes after he retired and shortly before 1 p.m. he left for lunch at his lodgings—on the A.6 road—at Elstow. He cut short his normal one hour lunch interval by half and was back at the Court at 1.35.

How the Bedfordshire Times & Standard *reported the appeal on 23 February 1962. The* Bedfordshire Times & Standard judge Hanratty only on the evidence they had heard, and if they did so they would have to acquit.

It took the jury over nine hours of debate and disagreement to reach their verdict. When they filed back into court it was almost a quarter past nine on Saturday night, 17 February 1962. Outside the Shire Hall, as word spread of the impending verdict, the huge crowds that had been steadily growing throughout the evening, surged toward the court building, then fell strangely silent. The reaction almost mirrored by those in the court where the silence was described as eerily tense. Then, as the foreman announced a guilty verdict, a loud, anguished cry from a woman at the back of the public gallery was heard above the gasps of horror that reverberated from all around the room. Hanratty stood and ran his tongue nervously between his lips as Mr Justice Gorman then pronounced the sentence of death.

From the court Hanratty was taken to the condemned cell at Bedford Prison and from there an appeal for clemency was launched. It failed despite 90,000 people signing the petition, and on the morning of 4 April he made the short walk from his cell to the scaffold, where he was executed by Harry Allen, still proclaiming his innocence.

From that moment on debate has raged over whether or not he was the man in the Morris Minor with Valerie Storie and Michael Gregston. Certainly his parents fought long and hard to clear his name, always believing in his innocence. Three Home Office inquiries have looked into the case: The first, in March 1967, the second in April 1975 and the third in May 1996, all upheld the verdict.

For most, Peter Alphon became a focus of their attention. He allegedly confessed to the murder shortly after Hanratty's execution and claimed he had been paid to kill Michael Gregston, but that the actual shooting had been accidental. The gun, according to Alphon, was then handed over to Charles France (Dixie). He, France, then disposed of the gun under the seat of the bus and placed two disused shells in the *Vienna* hotel. For France, claimed Alphon, it was a personal vendetta. In 1966, BBC's *Panorama* programme re-examined the case and Alphon's involvement. A year later he was then offered an interview with David Frost and later figured in books written about the Hanratty trial. But was he telling the truth? Charles France committed suicide two weeks before the execution so no one has ever been able to confirm or refute his story. That is until the discovery of DNA.

The exhibits used in the Bedford trial were, for a while lost, then re-discovered in 1991. DNA was then provided by the Hanratty family but the results proved inconclusive. Hanratty's body was then exhumed in 2001 in order that DNA could be extracted for the purposes of finally clearing him of the murder and rape. This was then compared with mucus found in the handkerchief that had been wrapped around the gun when discovered under the bus seat, and with semen preserved in the panties worn by Valerie Storie. The results showed that the samples matched Hanratty.

At the subsequent hearing these results were contested by the family on the grounds that there had been contamination to the exhibits. However, it was successfully argued at the time that if they were right then on the exhibits tested there ought to have been other male DNA present and there was not. Therefore, the appeal failed and the judgement meant that James Hanratty had almost certainly been guilty.

Index

Acott, Police Superintendent
   Robert 127–147
Adams, Hilde Maria 119
Adams, Sarah 18
Adams, Thomas 19
Alderson, Baron 11
Allen, Harry 146
Alphon, Peter 130, 144
Ampthill 84
Anderson, Louise 132, 139
Archer, Esther 27
Arsley Asylum, 64
Astle, Thomas 103, 105
Atwell, James 20
Atwell, John 20
Atwell, Sarah 20

Badger, William 19
Barron, Police Superintendent
   Charles 126
Bedford 11, 19, 25, 45, 50–53, 57,
   79, 81, 83, 86, 92, 98, 103,
   124, 129, 132, 144
Bedford Modern Boys School 86
Bedford Prison 10, 29, 59, 62–64,
   101, 106, 146
Bedford Times 21, 30, 38, 40, 60,
   107,
128, 135, 142, 145
Bennet, Police Constable 25
Benson, Patrick 30
Biggleswade 119
Billington, James (hangman) 65
Blackburn, Mr Justice 45
Blunham 90–91, 95
Blythe Place 74, 76
Bradbury, William 33–34, 37, 40
Bramwell, Baron 37
Bray, John 86
Bridge Farm 94
Boyd, John 101
Bull, William 45–47
Burgin, Effie 57
Burkett, William 70
Burrows, Able 15–22

Burrows, Francis 17–18
Burton, Sydney 126

Calcraft (hangman) 40
Caldecote, Lord 117–118
Cariss, Emma 42
Carver, Mary 6
Castle, Jane 23, 25–32
Castle, Joseph 25–32
Chequers Inn 9–11
Church Street 111
Clarke, Police Constable 69
Clophill 124
Cooke, Edwin 129
Corn Exchange 61–62
Covington, Arthur 58–65
Covington, George 57, 61, 64
Cromer Hyde 27

Day, James 33–35
Day, Mr Justice 62, 65
Dazley, Elizabeth 7, 12
Dazley, William 4, 6, 8–10, 13
Dorney Reach 122
Durant, Frederick 129–130

Eagles, Ezra 8, 10
Eggington 68
Ellis, Henry Samuel 48–49
Ellis, John (hangman) 72
Ellis, Samuel 48
Evans, Terry 142
Eynesbury 57, 62

France, Carol-Ann 131
France, Charles 131, 132, 138
France, Charlotte 131, 137

Galvez, Juliana 130
George Hotel 59
Glenister, Charity, 15, 17–19
Goodwin, Frank 90
Goodwin, Police Inspector 94
Gorman, Mr Justice 134, 146
Great Barford 92

Gregston, Janet 127
Gregston, Michael 122–147
Grey Friars 51

Hanratty, James 122–147
Harrow 123
Harpur Street 58
Hatfield 27
Havers, Mr Justice 120–121
Haynes Camp 79, 88
Haynes Village 86
Heath & Reach 15–16
Hedley, George 9–10
Hemming, Joseph 41, 43, 45–46
Henshaw, Police Constable 76
Hepburn, Sergeant Major 81–89
Heron Inn 25
Hockliffe 68
Holben, Police Constable 84
Hull, Florence 94
Hull, Priscilla 51–54
Hurst, Isaac 9

Iddesleigh Road 98
Ilford 129

Jacobin 15
James, Police Inspector 76
Jersey 81
Jolly Topers Inn 35
Jones, Grace 144

Kempston 48, 103
Kerr, John 126
Kinsey, Dr 64
Kirkham, Joshua 50

Langdale, Roy 135, 139, 143
Lawrence, Hon Sir Geoffrey 100
Leighton Buzzard 16, 66–67
Lewis, Dr Charles 77
Lilley 33–34, 39
Little Staunton 41, 43
Lowe, Ada 49
Lowe, Ellis 49–50
Lowe, Lucy 48–56
Lowe, Thomas 49
Luddington, Arthur 98–100
Luddington, Kenneth 98–102
Luton 25–27, 31, 33, 73–74, 109,
   111

MacKelvie, John 92
Major, Thomas 68
Manton, Bertie 109–118
Manton, Irene 109–118
Mardlin, Police Constable 54
Marshall, Eva 92, 95
Marshall, Lindsay 92, 94–97
Marshall, Sarah 41
Martin, Amy 73–78
Martin, Henry Charles 73–78
Mead, Jonas 4–6, 10
Mead, Simeon 4–6, 8, 10
Mills, Mr 31
Model Farm 23
Morgan, Police Superintendent 133
Morley, Arthur 98

New England Farm 4
Norman, Edith 92
Nudds, William 130, 137, 144

Old Station Inn 122
Oliver, Chief Inspector 119
Oliver, Dr 101
O'Malley, Mr 12–13
O'Sullivan, Richard 100

Phillips, Lieutenant Colonel 85
Plantation Road 69
Plough Inn 168
Plume of Feathers Inn 113
Pope, Superintendent 24, 37
Potton 6–7, 9
Prior, Dr 62
Purser, John 23
Pym, Francis 8

Queen Street 76

Railway Swan Inn 53
Rault, Ellen 79–89
Reeve, Harriett 66–72
Reeve, William 66–72
Regent Street 109
Reynolds, Edward 9
Reynolds, Sarah 4–14
Rhyl 142, 144
Richardson, Elizabeth 54
Riddy, Henry 48
Riddy, Lucy 48
Robinson, Ernest 103–108

Robinson, William 53
Roebuck Inn 68
Round Green 33–34, 36
Royal Oak 33
Ryan, Jim 130–132

Sandal, Dr Henry 6–7, 12
Shearman, Mr Justice 70
Sherrard, Michael 133, 140–141,
    144
Shields, Phyllis 119
Shire Hall 60, 71, 134, 146
Simpson, Keith 116
Singleton, Mr Justice 117
Skillett, John 129, 132, 138
Slough 122
South Mills Farm 92
Spread Eagle Inn 9
St Albans 124
St Georges Road 91–92
Stag Inn 67
Stagsden 48–49
Stagsden Side-Gate 53
Stanmore 123
Storie, Valerie 122–147
Stotfield 119
Sturges, Thomas 43–44
Summeries Castle 23
Swain, Dr Edward 64
Swanwick, Graham 135–136

Tadlow 4, 8
Taplow 122
Timms, Alfred 90–91

Toms, Jack 68
Tomson, Kit 37
Trower, James 129, 138
Turvey 53
Twiss, Reverend 10

Vienna Hotel 129–130, 137–138

Waldock, George 8
Ward, Arthur 116–117
Ware 26–27, 29
Welch, Levi 33–36
Welch, Mary Ann 36
Wellington Street 58
White Hart Inn 66, 68
Whitehill Farm 34–35
Whitworth, Ellen 29
Whitworth, Emily 28
Whitworth, Francis 27
Whyley, Gregory 96
Williams, Detective Constable 132
Williams, Dr J 119
Williams, Dr, Mervyn 120
Williams, Mr Justice 29
Wilstead Woods 79–80, 83, 86
Windsor 122
Woburn 16
Woodroffe, Police Inspector 9
Wootton 48–50, 56
Wright, Frederick 94

Yellowlees, Dr Henry 101
Yorke Street 27